Rebel on Pointe

UNIVERSITY PRESS OF FLORIDA

Florida A&M University, Tallahassee
Florida Atlantic University, Boca Raton
Florida Gulf Coast University, Ft. Myers
Florida International University, Miami
Florida State University, Tallahassee
New College of Florida, Sarasota
University of Central Florida, Orlando
University of Florida, Gainesville
University of North Florida, Jacksonville
University of South Florida, Tampa
University of West Florida, Pensacola

Lee Wilson

REBEL ON POINTE

A Memoir of Ballet & Broadway

University Press of Florida

Gainesville · Tallahassee · Tampa · Boca Raton

Pensacola · Orlando · Miami · Jacksonville · Ft. Myers · Sarasota

Library of Congress Control Number: 2014937649
ISBN 978-0-8130-6008-8

The University Press of Florida is the scholarly publishing agency for the State University System of Florida, comprising Florida A&M University, Florida Atlantic University, Florida Gulf Coast University, Florida International University, Florida State University, New College of Florida, University of Central Florida, University of Florida, University of North Florida, University of South Florida, and University of West Florida.

University Press of Florida
15 Northwest 15th Street
Gainesville, FL 32611-2079
http://www.upf.com

Contents

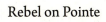

Rebel on Pointe

1 I Discover Dance,

1946–1954

I made my debut as a professional ballet dancer in a command performance for Prince Rainier and Princess Grace in Monte Carlo. I was sixteen years old, and dance was my passion. The year was 1962, and in the following years, I performed for ballet superstars in Paris, gun-toting revolutionaries in Algeria, American aristocrats at the Metropolitan Opera, and Mikhail Baryshnikov on Broadway. I worked with some of the great dancers and choreographers of the late twentieth century, including Rudolf Nureyev, Erik Bruhn, Alicia Markova, Alvin Ailey, and Michael Bennett. I performed leading roles, supporting roles, show-stealing roles, and as corps de ballet.

In the 1950s and 1960s, many people thought of dance as a pastime for pretty young girls before they settled down and got married, but for me, dance was the rare community where men and women were equally respected and equally paid. At a time when the majority of American women were housewives, dance gave me physical, emotional, and financial freedom.

It gave me a community that nurtured and inspired me. And while mainstream society reserved most of the good jobs for men, I lived in a community where women could and did rise to the top.

When I was a little girl, I was short, pudgy, and pigeon-toed. My parents didn't work in the arts, and I lived in the suburbs of the second-smallest state in the United States. Nevertheless, I decided to become a ballerina.

In New Castle, Delaware, during the 1950s, fathers worked and mothers stayed home. My family was no exception. Every weekday morning, Dad picked up his briefcase, kissed Mom goodbye, and left our white frame house in the suburbs. Mom stayed home with me and my three younger brothers, Trick, Twink, and Tuck.

Our neighborhood, five miles south of Wilmington, had Protestants and Catholics, working-class families and professionals. It didn't have people of color, people identified as gay, or women with high-profile jobs.

Many people remember the 1950s as the golden age of tranquility between World War II in the 1940s and the sexual revolution and civil rights movement in the 1960s, but I remember those years as the time when I realized that society stacked the deck against girls, and I began my search for a community where my gender would not define me as a second-class citizen.

While I was searching for my place in the dance community, there was a shift in American society and a transformation of American dance that brought mainstream society and the dance community closer together. But in the early 1950s, when I began my journey, the dance community was a world apart from the society into which I was born.

My dad was a chemist, and he loved his work. During World War II, while he was finishing his PhD, he helped develop the high-octane fuel that made American planes more efficient than the better-engineered German planes. After the war, he took a job with the DuPont company—a secure, lifelong job that gave him a good pension and lifetime health coverage for himself and his dependents. At first, he worked in the laboratories of the DuPont Experimental Station, but by the time my memories begin, he was working in the Nemours Building, one of the twin DuPont towers in downtown Wilmington. The DuPont towers were the tallest buildings in the city—fourteen stories high—and DuPont was a magic name in Delaware. The DuPont Highway ran up and down the state and was the corridor between New York and Washington, D.C. The DuPont Playhouse was the theatre where ballet and acting companies performed, and everyone knew the DuPont slogan, "Better things for better living . . . through chemistry."

Dad worked in the film department—not with movies, but with films like Mylar, which was used in the space program. I liked his scientific terminology. In our house, we didn't have plastic bags and plastic toys; we had polyethylene bags and polystyrene toys. When Dad watered the garden, he turned on the H_2O. One day, he brought home a large yellow fruit that we children identified as the largest grapefruit we had ever seen—but it wasn't a grapefruit. It was a lemon grown in a Mylar greenhouse. None of the girls at dance class could believe the huge fruit was a lemon until I cut it open and their mouths puckered from the juice.

Dad traveled to exotic cities like Buffalo, New York, and sent me picture postcards and handwritten letters from everywhere he went. At the beginning of each trip, Mom drove him to the airport, and the entire family walked Dad to the gate and watched the plane take off. In the early 1950s, when most people were stuck on the ground, Dad's job allowed him to fly.

His job not only gave him great satisfaction, it also gave him money. Dad never let us forget that it was *his* money that allowed us to have dance lessons and piano lessons and fried chicken with green beans rather than a dreary life with only bread and water. We all understood that Mom and the children were dependents on his tax return and dependent on his money.

Because Dad made the money, he decided how it should be spent. Sometimes he held a family vote, but everyone knew that children's votes didn't really count, and although Mom had an ace, Dad held the trump. One Saturday morning, Dad went out to buy a dishwasher—at least that's what Mom thought he went out to buy. She had been skimping and saving for months for a dishwasher, but Dad came home with a freezer. He decided that Mom did the dishes just fine and that a freezer would be more fun. He and the children could freeze fruits and vegetables from his garden. Mom was very quiet while the rest of the family celebrated the fact that we could now have four different kinds of ice cream at the same time.

I noticed that people were impressed when Dad stated his occupation on applications for Bible school or the YMCA. None of the applications had space for a wife's work. If women were mentioned at all, it was with the words "and Mrs." before their husbands' names.

I knew that Dad worked very hard because when he came home from work, he could do as he pleased while Mom made dinner. He could read the evening paper, listen to a symphony on the Magnavox, or help Trick and me perform backbends, cartwheels, and walkovers. After dinner, while Mom did the dishes and put Twink and Tuck to bed, Dad sat on the sofa with Trick on his right and me on his left and read wonderful stories: *Winnie the Pooh, Alice in Wonderland, Treasure Island, Kidnapped*, the *Iliad*, and the *Odyssey*. He read each character with a different voice, and, as he read, I traveled to new worlds in my imagination.

When I was eight, I didn't know how Dad actually spent his time when he was at work, but I knew exactly what my "non-working" mother did. She homeschooled me and seven-year-old Trick and made sure that we stayed at least one grade ahead of the private schools in every subject. She listened to three-year-old Twink read the Dick and Jane books while baby Tuck was napping. She did all of the cooking, cleaning, laundry, and ironing with no dishwasher and, before Twink was born, no clothes dryer. She baked chocolate cakes for the church bake sales and sewed costumes for dance recitals. She bought unfinished doors, painted them white, and attached black metal legs to make them into tables. She cut everyone's hair, including her own. She painted the walls, scrubbed the floors, and washed diapers in the toilet. I knew exactly what it meant when people "didn't work."

One Wednesday afternoon I was given the opportunity to see what my father did that brought him satisfaction, money, power, and respect. Most Wednesdays, I took the bus to and from choir practice at St. Andrew's Church in downtown Wilmington, but this particular Wednesday, Mom told me to walk to Dad's office so that he could drive me home. It was a sweltering afternoon, but I ran from the church to the Nemours Building.

When I entered the lobby, I felt a rush of cool air. Air conditioning! Dad was working in luxury while Mom sweltered at home. I took the elevator up to one of the top floors and found Dad's office. Dad's secretary, a sophisticated woman in high heels and lipstick, informed Dad that I had arrived and took me into his private office. In front of me was my dad at work: suit coat off, seated at his desk, Dad was reading the sports section of the Philadelphia *Bulletin*. Behind him, a plate-glass window showed the city at his feet. As Dad lowered the newspaper, his secretary asked, "Can I get you some more coffee?" In that moment, I knew that I wanted to be a person who worked.

The 1950s were a step backward for working women. During World War II, women performed many jobs previously reserved for men, and Rosie the Riveter was the inspiring symbol of women at work. But when the war was over, women were told it was their patriotic duty to quit their jobs and return to their families. Women who balked were fired. The women who had flown fighters and bombers for the Women Airforce Service Pilots were disbanded. No passenger airline would hire a female pilot. Even "female jobs" had restrictions: stewardesses had to be single and were forced to retire at the age of thirty or thirty-two, depending on the airline.

The Servicemen's Re-adjustment Act of 1944, also known as the GI Bill, guaranteed the dominance of men for at least a generation after the war. This bill provided that men and women who had served at least ninety days in the active military were entitled to scholarships for college and vocational training, unemployment benefits, and low-cost loans for homes, farms, and businesses. Since the active military was overwhelmingly male, this gave millions of men financial and educational advantages that most women didn't have. However, in our family, it was Mom who finished her master's degree on the GI Bill. During the war, Mom was an officer in U.S. Army Intelligence in Washington, D.C., where her job involved breaking codes. At the age of twenty-one, she was fluent in French, Spanish, English, Latin, and ancient Greek. She refused to tell me about her work because, she said, "Loose Lips Sink Ships," but when she was in her eighties, I learned that she had traveled around the country for the Army. I asked Mom if she had ever thought about pursuing a career, and she said, "No. At the end of the war, everybody told us how lucky we were not to have to work any more—how lucky we were to be able to stay home with our husbands and families." With sadness, she added, "And we believed them."

After the war, Mom finished her master's degree, married Dad, and had four children in less than eight years. It would be an additional eight years before she got out of the suburbs of Delaware.

Mom was as smart as Dad, and she was a brilliant motivator, but her choices in the mid-1940s were shaped by a fast-changing social and political landscape that made a non-working wife a status symbol and gave men tremendous advantages over women. Twenty years later, my dance career would be shaped by changes in the world of ballet: the demise of European-originated touring companies and the rise of a more stable, more patriarchal company in America. But I wasn't thinking of social and political events when I began to dance.

Trick and I began tap lessons when I was four and he was three. Mom didn't tell me at the time, but I was pigeon-toed, and our pediatrician told her that I should have corrective shoes or dance lessons. Mom thought that dance lessons would be less stigmatizing and more fun, so she found a woman in the neighborhood who gave tap lessons in her basement, and signed us up for classes once a week.

From the very first class, I loved to tap: *Shuffle step. Shuffle step. Flap ball change. Stomp. Step clap. Step clap. Flap ball change. Stomp.* I loved the scraping sound of taps brushing across the cement floor, the clicking sounds of the heel taps, and the crash of a full-footed stomp. Even the words were fun to say: "shuffle" and "flap." When no one was looking, Trick and I used to face each other and say, "flap, flap, flap," sticking out our tongues on every flap.

During the class, Mom sat in a corner of the basement and wrote down every new step. When we got home, she had us perform the entire routine and made sure we didn't forget anything. The bedroom Trick and I shared had a carpet, so Mom went to Sears and bought a roll of linoleum. Every afternoon, Trick would grab one end, I'd grab the other, and we'd roll out the dance floor and tap.

After a year of tap, I was still pigeon-toed, so Mom decided that I should study ballet, a dance form based on turnout (swiveling the toes away from the body—the opposite of pigeon-toed). The school she chose was the Joyce Potter School of Dancing in downtown Wilmington. According to the school's brochure, Joyce Potter had trained three girls who danced with the Rockettes and had other students who had appeared on the Paul Whiteman and Ted Mack television shows. She had a large, air-conditioned studio with mirrors along one wall and dressing rooms for the young dancers. My once-a-week, afternoon class had fifteen girls and lasted one hour, with ballet first, tap second, and acrobatics at the end. All of the girls had to wear pink cotton jumpers, which our mothers washed and ironed every week.

At the first class, the teacher, who was not Joyce Potter, showed us the five basic positions. However, basic didn't mean easy. For first position, we put our heels together and swiveled our toes out as far as possible. Ideally, our feet would form a horizontal line, an angle of one hundred and eighty degrees. My feet barely made ninety. The most difficult of the five positions was fifth position. Imagine first position with the right foot slid in front of the left, so that the right heel is touching the big toe of the left foot, and the little toe of the right foot is touching the heel of the left foot. The position seemed impossible, but as the teacher repeated the words, "heel to toe," I remembered my father's advice: "If at first you don't succeed, look at the problem from a different point of view." I realized that I could accomplish the goal of having a big toe against one heel and a little toe against the other by swiveling my toes *in*. Soon, my right toes were pointing left, and my left toes were pointing right. As I reveled in my success, the teacher informed me that I had to start over and turn my toes *out*.

I wanted to skip the ballet portion of the class, but the brochure clearly stated that although acrobatic dance was optional, ballet was mandatory. Ballet was "the foundation of all dance—and it is that requirement that has made this school famous for its graceful tap and acrobatic dancers."

This requirement for girls, this "foundation of all dance," wasn't even an option for boys. Trick's class, the boys' class, had one full hour of tap and acrobatics. Boys who liked ballet were often teased and called "sissies," and more than one father told his boy, "No son of mine is going to prance around in tights." In the movies, some female dancers, like Leslie Caron and Cyd Charisse, were ballet dancers, and others, like Ann Miller and Debbie Reynolds, were tap dancers, but the male stars, including Fred Astaire, Gene Kelly, and the Nicholas Brothers, were all tap dancers.

The role models that Mom chose for Trick and me were Marge and Gower Champion. I hadn't seen them dance, but Mom told me that they were a famous dance team who performed both on stage and on film. Once a week, in addition to our group classes, Trick and I had a half-hour private tap lesson.

The dance year climaxed with the spring recital at the DuPont Playhouse. In 1952, when I was six, Joyce Potter presented *The Alice in Wonderland Revue*. Trick and I were the tap-dancing mushrooms that made Alice grow taller and shorter. Almost all the mothers knew how to sew, and the costumes were quite elaborate. Our mushroom costumes were dark brown satin covered with gold mesh, and had sequin-decorated gold satin collars and cuffs. Our hats, shaped like coolie hats, were also gold satin with swirls of dark brown sequins. Each hat had a one-inch, rectangular gold satin pillow which snapped on and off. To grow tall, Alice would unsnap the tiny pillow on Trick's hat and pretend to pop it into her mouth. Then she would disappear behind the set, and a taller, identically-dressed Alice would emerge a moment later. To grow smaller, Alice did the same routine with my little pillow. There were a total of three Alices, and Trick and I tapped onto the stage to provoke each growth spurt up or down.

I loved performing. I loved the sets, the lights, the music, the costumes, and having the important job of making Alice shrink—even though I knew it wasn't real.

In this recital, I also performed a ballet number with my class of fifteen girls. We were collectively the birthday cake at the Mad Hatter's tea party. Our costumes were pink and white tutus, and on our heads we each wore a pillbox hat with a fabric candle sticking up in the middle.

The dance included pas de bourrées, which the teacher called back-side-front. (I would later learn that there are many kinds of pas de bourrées, and they are not all back-side-front.) In the recital, as the class pas de bourréed left, the biggest girl pas de bourréed right and bumped the girl next to her. As the class pas de bourréed right, the big girl pas de bourréed left and bumped the girl on the other side. Throughout the dance, my hat kept slipping to one side, so every time I did a little bourrée turn, I shoved the hat and hoped that no one would notice. At the end of the dance, we all ran into the wings where our mothers held big cardboard boxes shaped and decorated to look like pieces of a round birthday cake. We pulled off our hats, ducked under the wedge-shaped boxes, and scooted back onto the stage. When all of the pieces of cake came together to form a big, round cake, the stage lights went out, and the cake lit up—all except one piece which covered the biggest girl in the class. In the wings, the grandmother of the big girl explained to the other mothers, "Those wires got in my granddaughter's way, so I just pulled them out!" Mom laughed out loud, but Joyce Potter was furious and informed everyone within earshot that when she and her dancers were working to create an effect, no one, neither dancer nor mother, had the right to destroy the effect.

During my second year at Joyce Potter's, I got my first pair of toe shoes, Capezio Duro-Toe. The school recommended Duro-Toe because the shank of the shoe, the support running the length of the shoe, was the strongest of all the models, so it would give the girls' feet the greatest support and would last the entire year. At first, I hated the toe shoes. In spite of my bunny pads (little mittens of bunny fur that covered my toes), the shoes gave me blisters. But as the shoes softened, and my feet grew tougher, I began to enjoy walking around on my toes. I was small for my age, and the shoes measured only six inches from the back of the heels to the tips of the toes, but I felt tall and regal whenever I went on pointe.

Some of the mothers were concerned about putting their daughters on pointe at such a young age and feared that the girls might suffer injuries, but I didn't hear of any injuries, and my own feet became very strong. Within a few years, I could stand on pointe even in ballet slippers.

Joyce Potter's recital in 1954 was a double bill of *Peter Pan* and *Coppélia*. By this time, I was taking a half-hour private toe lesson as well as the private tap lesson with Trick, and I was cast as Tinker Bell in *Peter Pan*. As soon as Joyce

Potter told me that the bed in the Darling nursery would be a trampoline, I began taking trampoline lessons at the YWCA so I could do a joyful somersault after my entrance and could exit by "flying" out the window head first into the wings, where two men would catch me.

Unfortunately, the Monday before the recital, during the playtime at the end of my weekly Brownie meeting, a boy on the playground pushed me off a merry-go-round-type apparatus. Instead of letting go and rolling away, I clung to the bars, determined to get back on. My right knee dragged across the gravel and began gushing blood. The Brownie troupe leader picked me up and drove me to the emergency room. As the doctor examined the bloody gash, I told him about my dance recital that weekend, and he assured me that I would be able to dance. He threaded a needle with black thread, and I squeaked in alarm, "Black! The entire audience will see that! Don't you have pink?!" But thread color was not negotiable. The doctor insisted that the thread had to be black so that he could find it to cut it out when my knee had healed.

Two days later, the day of the dress rehearsal, my knee still bled every time I moved. Mom called Joyce Potter to tell her that I wouldn't be able to dance, and I agreed to lend my costume to another girl. Mrs. Potter said that she wanted to express her appreciation to me for lending the costume by telling the audience what had happened and calling me on stage for a bow at the end of the recital.

That Friday night, I watched the show from the balcony. My dance number was cut, but the new Tinker Bell did all of the staging, and I saw how easily a dancer could be replaced. At the end of the show, Joyce Potter called me onto the stage, but as I began to curtsey, I realized that my right knee wouldn't bend. What I thought was gracefully, but was probably excruciatingly slowly, I straightened my right leg behind me and pointed my toes. Then I did a rond de jambe (literally, circle of leg), so that my right leg was pointed in front of me. As I bowed from the waist, Joyce Potter bumped me with her hip to provoke my exit, and I scampered with a limp into the wings.

I had been on stage for only a few minutes, but I had learned two things. First, never go on stage without rehearsing—no matter how simple the steps might seem—or you might be embarrassed. Dancers can't control every-

thing that happens on stage because sets, props, costumes, and other dancers don't always function as they should, but there is no excuse for failing to
rehearse. Second, if you haven't earned the applause, you feel like a fraud. If
anyone took a bow for the costume, it should have been Mom. As I stood in
the wings that evening, I resolved that the next time I went on stage, and the
next, and the next, I would do something to earn the applause.

In 1953, the year between these two recitals, my aunt Jean invited me to
see my first professional ballet, the Slavenska-Franklin Ballet, which starred
Mia Slavenska, Frederic Franklin, and Alexandra Danilova. I was still much
more interested in tap than ballet, but I was delighted by the prospect of an
evening out without my parents. I dressed in my Sunday best, and when we
arrived at the DuPont Playhouse, the anticipation of the crowd reminded
me of the Christmas Eve church service at St. Andrew's, my favorite service
of the year. The lobby of the theatre was jammed. Everyone was dressed up,
talking, and laughing, and the excitement of the audience was contagious.

Jean and I walked down the aisle and settled into our seats in the orchestra
section, and I had the same feeling of awe and wonder that I had in church.
In church, I looked up at the altar, up at the lectern, up at the pulpit, and up
at the stained glass windows. In the theatre, I looked up at the red velvet curtain trimmed with gold, up at the balcony, up at the sparkling chandeliers,
and up at the stage. The dominant color of the theatre, like church, was red.
It was all comfortably familiar. My paternal grandfather, Reverend Joseph
Durant Cooper Wilson (Gampie to his grandchildren), was an Episcopal
minister who had served at the church where President Franklin Delano
Roosevelt had worshiped when he was in Georgia. My dad, Joseph Durant
Cooper Wilson II, was on the vestry of St. Andrew's Episcopal Church in
Wilmington, and my brothers and I went to Bible school, Sunday school,
and church. My family said grace before meals, prayers before bed, and gave
up candy for Lent. On my windowsill, I had a cross that absorbed sunlight
during the day and glowed at night, and my family had a series of books
about the miraculous lives of the saints. The church provided me with music, ritual, pageantry, and stories that transcended the everyday world.

On that February night at the Slavenska-Franklin Ballet, I sensed that ballet, like church, could be a transcendent experience. As the lights dimmed, instead of one solitary organ, an entire orchestra began to play. When the curtain rose, the dancers leaped onto the stage, which was far more exciting than the predictable slow march of clergy and choir in their predictable red and white vestments. At the ballet, the costumes sparkled, and the sets were different for each ballet. In *The Nutcracker Suite*, there were dancers from exotic locations—Arabia, Russia, and China—and the beautiful Sugar Plum Fairy was the queen of the realm. This ballerina queen in her sparkling tutu was different from all other queens I had ever seen: she wasn't born into her position; she had earned it. She was the queen because she was an extraordinary dancer. Her position, unlike that of other queens, was one that little girls from the suburbs could realistically hope to attain. That night at the ballet, I caught a glimpse of a better world for women, and in time, I would realize I had found an art that nourished my soul.

For the next seven years, Mom bought tickets for every ballet company that came to Wilmington or Philadelphia. As soon as an advertisement appeared in the newspapers, we would sit down together and choose which ballets and which dancers we wanted to see. From the balcony of the Du-Pont Playhouse, and from the peanut gallery of the Academy of Music, I saw the Sadler's Wells Ballet (which became the Royal Ballet in 1956), the London Festival Ballet (now the English National Ballet), the Royal Danish Ballet, the New York City Ballet, Ballet Russe, and Ballet Theatre (which became American Ballet Theatre in 1957). The more I went to the ballet, and the more I learned about the dance community, the more I realized how different it was from the society I knew.

In our community, and in much of America, the most important social organization was the church. Everyone in our neighborhood, and everyone in my school, when I eventually went to school, worshiped the same omnipotent God, and He was male. The hierarchy of the Christian church was male—ministers, priests, bishops, cardinals, and popes. Women in cinched-waist dresses and high heels were allowed to serve juice and cookies in the basement, but only men in vestments could serve wine and wafers in the chancel. Ministers in pulpits drew parallels between our Father who ruled in Heaven and our fathers who presided in our homes. Spiritual advisors to government officials were male, and in 1954, the church flexed its power to add the words "under God" to the Pledge of Allegiance. In government, in church, and at home, men made and enforced the laws which gave them power. Once in a moment of frustration, Mom muttered to me: "Gampie thinks he's God, so you know who your father thinks *he* is." I understood her frustration because I felt it too.

I was the firstborn, but I wasn't the namesake because that honor could only go to a boy. Trick was the namesake, Joseph Durant Cooper Wilson III, and he, Twink, and Tuck would all be links between past and future generations of Wilsons. I was a temporary Wilson—a Wilson only until I married, at which time the government would automatically change my name, and I would become Mrs. Somebody Else. Even at a young age, I knew the importance of establishing a brand name. I knew that boys could build an identity over a lifetime and could benefit from the reflected glory of earlier generations in a way that girls could not. I knew that by changing their names, women became invisible.

But as I watched one ballet company after another, I realized that female dancers took control of their names. During the first half of the twentieth century, Russian dancers were the most revered, so many Western dancers changed their names to sound Russian. The British dancer Lilian Alicia Marks became the great ballerina Alicia Markova. And ballerinas didn't give up their names when they married. When Maria Tallchief, prima ballerina with the New York City Ballet, married choreographer George Balanchine, she kept her birth name—a name that proudly proclaimed her American Indian heritage.

In ballet, women didn't defer to the men. In fact, the men partnered the women, which allowed the women to execute more pirouettes and balance on pointe longer than they could without support. The men in ballet lifted the women into the air to soar higher than they could by themselves. Female dancers usually got first billing and the last curtain calls. The most popular ballets of my childhood, *Swan Lake, Coppélia, Sleeping Beauty, Giselle,* and *The Nutcracker,* were all about women. And the women in these ballets didn't disguise themselves as men, like writers George Sand and George Eliot and the Brontë sisters. They didn't dress up as boys to get into the action.

They were unapologetically female. Ballet gave me a glimpse of a different world order, and I wanted to be a part of that world.

As a child, I was blissfully ignorant of how difficult it is to become a professional ballet dancer. In the 1950s, the regional companies that dot the country today didn't exist. There were three major companies in America, all based in New York, and many of the jobs in those companies were taken by foreign dancers who had fled Europe during World War II. There were far more jobs for American boys in Major League Baseball than for American girls in major ballet companies. I didn't know then that training to become an elite ballet dancer is like training for the Olympics: there are many obstacles along the way, but the biggest problem is simply that the odds of success are so slim.

What were the odds that a short, pigeon-toed girl in the suburbs of Delaware could compete with physically gifted girls training in the company schools in New York? In the 1950s, aspiring dancers couldn't watch videotapes to learn new techniques, steps, or roles. I saw great dancers every few months from the fifth balcony of the Academy of Music. Girls in New York saw great dancers every day in the rehearsal studios. As a child, I didn't know that the economics of ballet would determine which dancers got hired, or that government regulations would dictate where I could dance.

Mom, my sole sounding board, never suggested that getting into a world-class ballet company might be difficult. From time to time, she simply reminded me that because I was short, I would probably have to be good enough to be a soloist before I could join a company. But Mom seemed as confident of my ability to become a professional dancer as she was of my ability to learn how to make my bed or multiply fractions, so when I was a child, I never considered the odds.

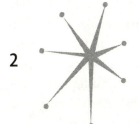

2　My Formative Teachers,
1954–1957

The fall I was eight, Mom asked Joyce Potter to put me into the advanced class, and Joyce Potter refused. Mom told me that Mrs. Potter was more interested in the uniform height of her class than in my progress as a dancer, so Mom took Trick and me to Anna Marie's Dance Studio, another school in downtown Wilmington.

Anna Marie was particularly good at tap and agreed with Mom that I needed the challenge of the advanced class. However, she thought I was too young and too small to perform with that class in the recital. She suggested that I also take the class with girls my own age as her guest and perform with that class in the recital. Mom and I were delighted. I now had four classes a week—two group classes, the private ballet lesson, and the private tap lesson with Trick. All of my classes were taught by Anna Marie herself.

Anna Marie was everybody's second mom. Her receptionist, Mrs. Steppi, had two daughters, one my age and one older, who became, respectively, a friend and our favorite babysitter. Anna Marie attended conferences with the National Association of Dance and Affiliated Artists and came home with new dance steps and new ideas for props, and her enthusiasm fueled our own. She showed us pictures in *Dance Magazine* so that we could see the perfect form we were trying to achieve. When ballet companies came to town, we all went to different performances and compared notes afterwards.

This dance community at the studio was particularly important to me because I didn't go to school, and my brothers and I were all trained to work independently at home. I enjoyed the benefits of homeschooling: I could do all of my academic work, plus my dance and piano practice, plus my private lessons during school hours. I never had to sit in a classroom while the teacher droned on about something I already knew. I could set my own schedule every day, and I had an academic hiatus for vacations, visits from relatives, and illness, so the class never moved ahead without me. However, I missed the camaraderie of school. I missed having friendships with children outside the family. Now, with four classes a week at Anna Marie's, I was becoming part of a community that was larger than my own family.

At the Slavenska-Franklin Ballet, I had sensed that dance empowered women, but at Joyce Potter's and Anna Marie's, I saw the empowerment up close. Joyce Potter and Anna Marie were not teachers for hire, like schoolteachers who answered to the men above them. Joyce Potter and Anna Marie ran their own businesses with their own names on the marquee, and they had the power to hire and fire their assistants and receptionists. When Joyce Potter produced and directed and choreographed her recitals, she was the boss. Mothers, fathers, stagehands, and lighting designers all took orders from her. Anna Marie had more joie de vivre than Joyce Potter, but she was also a person who took charge, and when Anna Marie's husband came to visit at the studio, he was a welcome and beloved guest, but Anna Marie was still the boss.

One afternoon when I was ten, after my private ballet lesson, Anna Marie told Mom and me that she had taught me almost everything she knew about ballet. She said that I'd continue to improve in her classes, but she thought I should supplement them with classes taught by someone who specialized in ballet. Anna Marie had done some research and learned that Maria Swoboda, a New York teacher who had danced with the Bolshoi Ballet in

Moscow, was giving ballet classes on Saturdays at the Philadelphia YWCA. She suggested that Mom and I check out the classes.

The next Saturday morning, Mom and I took the train to the 30th Street Station in downtown Philadelphia and walked to the YWCA. Mom told me to remember the route because if I liked the class, I would travel alone the following week.

When we entered the YWCA, we were directed to a huge room filled with much older girls. Madame Swoboda told Mom that she didn't allow children in the class, but Mom convinced her to let me take this one class because we had traveled so far, so I changed into my leotard and found a place at the barre. (The word "barre" is used to describe both the handrail which runs the length of the studio, and the portion of the class which is performed holding onto the barre.)

Madame Swoboda pointed to a girl across the room and told me to follow her. I couldn't imagine why I would follow another girl—until the class began. Madame Swoboda did not demonstrate the combinations at the barre in advance. She had a set barre (sometimes called a fixed barre). In a set barre, the content and order of the exercises is exactly the same in every class, and the students are expected to have it memorized. Proponents of a set barre say it is efficient because dancers don't have to waste time learning the next exercise, and it allows students to concentrate on *how* they are executing the steps because they don't have to think about which step comes next. It also requires less work on the part of the teacher who doesn't have to create a new barre every day. (Many years later, I took class from a teacher in Paris who didn't even enter the studio until the end of the barre.)

However, there are several drawbacks. Dancers can get bored doing the exact same thing day after day and may put their brains and bodies on autopilot. The teacher can't tailor the exercises to address the dancers' weaknesses, nor can she introduce a new step at the barre and build upon it later in the class. Also, a set barre is difficult for new students and visitors because they have to keep their eyes on someone else and are always half a beat behind. Dancing *with* the music is inspiring and uplifting. Dancing *behind* the music is debilitating. That Saturday, an additional problem for me was that Madame Swoboda pronounced the French terminology with a Russian accent, and I was used to French terminology with an American accent. I couldn't understand half of what she was saying.

Fortunately, in the center (away from the barre), the combinations were new in each class, and I was able to see them before I had to perform them. Madame Swoboda's combinations were a revelation. At Anna Marie's, we faced front, side, or back. We pointed our feet front, side, or back. At Madame Swoboda's, there were angles, and they all had French names: *éffacé en avant, écarté en arrière*. Angles weren't just a matter of style. They were actual positions. I had to imagine that I was standing in a square so that I could create positions that were forty-five degrees from straight front. I couldn't just point my feet at the corner of the room because the room wasn't square, and every dancer had to have the same angle regardless of where she was placed in the room.

Madame Swoboda gave several combinations that began at the back of the studio and moved forward. When the first line reached the front of the studio, the line split in half, and half of the girls peeled off to the right and half to the left. Then the girls filed to the back of the room behind the rows moving forward and formed a new line. The music continued and the lines moved forward until Madame Swoboda indicated that she was ready to move on to the next combination. This pattern is not only efficient in the studio, with no time wasted between groups, but it can also be very effective on stage because the dancers peeling off in the front can exit into the front wings, run to the back wings, enter at the back of the stage, and move forward so that there seems to be an endless stream of dancers—far more than there actually are.

At Joyce Potter's and Anna Marie's, I had set the pace for children. At Madame Swoboda's, I had to keep up with the adults beside me and avoid being trampled by the adults behind me. It didn't matter that I was a foot shorter than many of the other girls. I had to cover the same ground. In a line of dancers, if one dancer leaps from a less-than-perfect position or lands on a less-than-turned-out foot, many in the audience won't notice, but if a single dancer juts out of line or holds up traffic so that the dancers behind her collide like a row of dominos, everyone will notice and everyone will know who is at fault. In Madame Swoboda's class, my first obligation was to travel at the same speed as the other dancers—a critical skill for ballerinas as well as members of the corps de ballet.

At the end of the class, all of the students applauded the teacher—a tradition that expresses the students' appreciation for the teacher's sharing her experience, and also acknowledges that teaching is the performance of older dancers. As Madame Swoboda bowed to the applause, I thought about how much I had learned in just one class. I had taken my first set barre. I had discovered new angles and new terminology, and I had learned a new pattern: moving forward, peeling off, running to the rear, and moving forward. As the applause ended, I walked over to Madame Swoboda and thanked her for allowing me to take the class. "Will I see you next week?" she asked. I was momentarily speechless. I felt like Cinderella with her fairy godmother. I was still dressed in rags, but I was invited to the ball.

During the next year, every Saturday morning, while Mom took the boys to tap class at Anna Marie's, Dad took me to the train station where I bought a child's round-trip ticket to Philadelphia for sixty-five cents. In my pocket, I had an additional twenty-five cents: fifteen cents for hot chocolate and a donut at the drug store before class and ten cents to call home if I missed the return train.

I loved taking the train. Some people stayed downstairs in the waiting room until the train was announced, but rain or shine, I went up onto the platform as soon as I had my ticket. People dressed up to take the train, and I admired their elegant dresses, suits, and coats. Over the loudspeaker, I'd hear the thrilling, booming voice of the conductor as he announced the arrival of the train. Soon I'd hear the rumble of the train in the distance. Then I'd see the jet-black engine, and finally, as the train slowed, the engine and the front cars would roll past me. The most glamorous car was the club car, which had individual seats that swiveled. The people who occupied these seats could swivel toward the window to look outside or swivel toward the interior of the car to face each other. These seats were occupied by men in suits, who read newspapers and sipped coffee on the trip north, and sipped scotch on the way home.

The next most interesting car was the dining car, which had white fabric tablecloths and napkins. Dad told me that the food was excellent on the train, but it was very expensive. I thought it must be wonderful to be so rich that you could eat an entire meal on a train. As the front cars passed by, I wondered where the people had gotten on. Baltimore? Washington, D.C.? Were they senators and congressmen, or were they artists? Were they going to the 30th Street Station? New York? Boston? Were they traveling on business, or were they going to see family and friends? When the train stopped, I climbed up two or three steps to get into a car at the back of the train. The passenger cars had rows of seats for two passengers on both sides of the center aisle. The seats faced both directions, and I'd try to get a window seat facing forward. For the entire journey to and from Philadelphia, I'd mind my posture to be worthy of riding the train. I watched the countryside roll by and admired the oil refineries that shot flames into the air. I loved the way the conductors announced the cities—especially "WILL-ming-ton, WILL-ming-ton" as we approached the Delaware station where Dad would be waiting for me downstairs in the car. Dance was already fulfilling my goal of seeing the world.

During this year with Madame Swoboda, I began to acquire a Russian technique. I also caught a glimpse of the professional world by listening to the girls in the dressing room. Some of them lived in New York and took the train down to Philadelphia on Saturdays. They talked about teachers and choreographers and auditions in New York. Most of the names they mentioned were unfamiliar to me, but I got a sense that there was a community of dancers larger than each individual studio and that although there was competition, it was friendly competition. And I looked forward to becoming part of that community.

Besides studying with Madame Swoboda, the other big event of that year was that Dad bought a television set. This exposed me to a wider world of dance that included not only world-class tap and ballet, but also jazz and musical theatre. In the late 1950s and early 1960s, dance was everywhere on television—on variety shows and in movies rerun on TV.

Every Sunday night, *The Ed Sullivan Show* featured dancers, singers, and musical groups, and everyone in my family would gather in our new playroom to watch. On one show, Galina Ulanova, a star of the Bolshoi Ballet, gave a heart-breaking performance of *The Dying Swan*. I could see the life draining out of her body and the subtle, final movements of her fingers that I could never have seen from the fifth balcony of the Academy of Music.

I saw the New York City Ballet production of *The Nutcracker* with George Balanchine as Drosselmeyer. I watched Shirley Temple and Bill "Bojangles" Robinson tap dance on a staircase in *The Little Colonel*. I saw *The Red Shoes*, the Rockettes, and the June Taylor Dancers. But my favorite dancing was in the musicals with Fred Astaire and Gene Kelly. Fred Astaire had superb technique and a seemingly infinite variety of props, including drum sets, a coat rack, and firecrackers. His dance on the ceiling in *Royal Wedding* was a marvel of creativity, but I couldn't really see myself dancing with Fred Astaire because he was so perfect and all of his partners were so glamorous. On the other hand, I *could* imagine myself dancing with Gene Kelly. (I knew, of course, that by the time I was old enough to dance professionally, he might have stopped dancing, but I wasn't going to let reality interfere with my fantasy.) Gene Kelly's choreography was as inventive as Fred Astaire's, but Gene Kelly wore sweaters and slacks instead of suits and tuxedos. He had a more exuberant, boy-next-door style, and I already knew that I was growing up to be Debbie Reynolds, not Ginger Rogers.

However, my visions of dancing with Gene Kelly came to a halt when Mom told me there was no future in tap. She said there were no tap companies, and the best tap movies were from the 1940s. She said the era of movie musicals was ending, but ballet was eternal. I thought performing with Gene Kelly might be more fun, but I trusted Mom to know what was best.

Dad warned me that ballet dancers were poorly paid, and I knew that Dad, even with a PhD and a good job, was always worried about money, but I also knew that I didn't want the expensive things he had. I didn't want a house with a mortgage or five dependents. I wanted to take ballet class in the morning and dance at the Metropolitan Opera House or Covent Garden in the evening. I wanted to see the world as a dancer on tour. I wanted to work with great artists—dancers who could not only thrill me with technical skills, but also create characters that touched my heart and made me laugh or cry. Other than ballet, all I needed to be happy was food, a few clothes, and a room of my own.

I was passionate about dance the way Dad was passionate about chemistry. I believed in dance both as a means of personal fulfillment and as a positive force in society. I liked the physical feeling of dance and the classical music that accompanied dance classes. I liked knowing that no matter what might happen in my life, I could go to ballet class, and for the next hour and a half, I could focus on the pursuit of perfection, a goal I could never attain—a goal that would last me a lifetime. I believed then, and I believe now, that dance is a force for good. It is an art in which people work together toward a common goal. Unlike sports, dance has no losers. It is good for the body and good for the brain. Like painting and music, dance transcends language. It unifies people of different races, creeds, and nationalities. In the 1950s and 1960s, many schools and churches were segregated, but on stage and on screen, I saw black dancers and white dancers working side by side. I wanted to live my life in this more inclusive world.

I began to look at ballet companies to see where I might fit in once I had a high school diploma. There were five companies I particularly admired: the Royal Ballet, the Royal Danish Ballet, Ballet Russe, Ballet Theatre, and the New York City Ballet. The Royal Ballet performed more of the classic story ballets than any of the American companies, and I liked the fact that it was based in London, but the biggest attraction was Margot Fonteyn, my favorite ballerina. Other dancers had stronger techniques and higher extensions (they lifted their legs higher), but, for me, Margot Fonteyn could create magic like no other dancer. In *Swan Lake*, I loved the way she played the dual role of Odette (the White Swan) and Odile (the Black Swan). Her White Swan had warmth and fragility, and her Black Swan retained enough humanity for the Prince not to realize that the Black Swan was a different girl—an imposter who was luring him into disaster. As Odile, Fonteyn couldn't always finish the thirty-two fouettés (a series of spins on one leg, which are the greatest technical challenge of the ballet), but she spun out of them so gracefully that it almost didn't matter. Margot Fonteyn inspired me from a distance, and I wanted to see her up close.

Another company I admired was the Royal Danish Ballet, which also had the glamour of being based in a foreign country. This company had produced the international star Erik Bruhn, who was the personification of elegance with a pure, classical technique. But the Royal Danish Ballet had only blonde Danes, so I thought this company an unlikely prospect for me.

In the United States, there were three important companies, and they were all based in New York: Ballet Russe, Ballet Theatre, and the New York City Ballet. Ballet Russe and Ballet Theatre toured the world and had a diverse repertory that included some of the great story ballets, such as *Coppélia*, *Giselle*, *Romeo and Juliet*, and *Swan Lake*. I wanted to dance all of these ballets.

In *Coppélia*, I wanted to dance the first act variation in which the ballerina tries unsuccessfully to get the attention of Coppélia, who she later discovers is an animated doll. In the second act, she impersonates the doll, and I wanted to perform the jerky movements that make the audience laugh.

Giselle requires a more mature dancer with grace, control, and acting ability. The title character is a peasant girl who falls in love with a young man, only to find out that he is a Prince engaged to someone else. His betrayal drives her into madness, and she dies. In the second act, the Prince comes to her grave to beg forgiveness, and Giselle rises from her grave as a spirit and protects him from the Wilis, the spirits of jilted girls who compel the men who jilted them to dance themselves to death. I particularly wanted to dance the mad scene.

Romeo and Juliet is based on the eponymous Shakespeare play. Juliet begins as a skittish young girl, becomes an enthusiastic young lover, and ends as a devastated widow who kills herself to join her husband in death. I loved the range of emotions in this ballet.

However, my favorite ballet, the *King Lear* of ballet, was *Swan Lake*. A Prince sets out to hunt a swan, and, as night falls, he sees the Swan Queen, Odette, transform into a girl. The swans are girls who have been bewitched by an evil magician who allows them human form at night. Only true love can break his spell. In a lyrical pas de deux, the Prince and Odette fall in love. However, the magician transforms his own daughter, Odile (the Black Swan), into a double for Odette (the White Swan). Odile dazzles the Prince with her thirty-two fouettés, and he, believing she is Odette, declares his love for Odile. The Prince soon realizes his mistake, and he and Odette jump into the lake and drown—an act that breaks the spell, kills the magician, and allows Odette and the Prince to ascend into heaven. (There are many variations on the ending of this ballet, including tragic endings.) Odette and Odile are played by the same dancer, so only Odile's black tutu distinguishes them physically, but emotionally they are worlds apart. For me, *Swan Lake* was the Mount Everest that a dancer had to climb to be considered a great ballerina.

These story ballets and more modern works by Jerome Robbins, Antony Tudor, and Agnes de Mille made Ballet Russe and Ballet Theatre very attractive.

The New York City Ballet (NYCB) was the third American company I knew. This company had been co-founded by George Balanchine who also co-founded the School of American Ballet (SAB), a feeder school for the company. I admired some of the dancers in the New York City Ballet, especially Maria Tallchief and Melissa Hayden, but with the exception of *The Nutcracker*, the NYCB did not perform any of the romantic full-length ballets. The NYCB programs I had seen in theatres were composed of several short ballets, nearly all choreographed by George Balanchine, and his ballets were often performed in leotards and tights without sets or stories. The dancers looked well-trained, but I wasn't alone in thinking that Balanchine ballets were cold. I could admire the geometry and the execution of the movements, but I preferred stories with flesh-and-blood characters, sets, and costumes. I liked ballets with passion, humor, and history. Great ballerinas like Karsavina, Markova, Fonteyn, and Tallchief had danced *Swan Lake* and *Giselle*, and I wanted to be part of that tradition. I also wanted to perform ballets by a diverse group of choreographers, so I zeroed in on three companies: the Royal Ballet, Ballet Russe, and Ballet Theatre.

However, the optimism and the confidence I had at age eleven were squashed by the time I turned twelve.

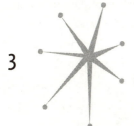

3   Dance Requires Grit,

1957–1959

Madame Swoboda's year in Philadelphia came to an end, and Mom moved me to the Philadelphia Dance Academy, a school established and directed by Nadia Chilkovsky, a modern dancer. The Philadelphia Dance Academy was associated with the Philadelphia Musical Academy and had an Undergraduate Program and a Preparatory Program. The Undergraduate Program, a college program, included modern dance, classical ballet, repertory, dance notation, history of the dance, piano, theory, improvisation, composition, harmony, pedagogy, and academic courses. The Preparatory Program offered modern dance, classical ballet, improvisation, dance composition, and dance notation.

Mom enrolled me for one ballet class a week while I was still studying tap and ballet with Anna Marie. My class was on Thursday afternoons, and it ended after dark, so the school insisted that I take a taxi back to the Suburban Station, even though I had made the one-mile walk earlier in the day. Taxis were one more expense added to the cost of lessons, trains, leotards, tights, tap shoes, ballet shoes, toe shoes, and recital costumes. I worried that Dad would hate me for wasting his money if I took dance lessons for ten or twelve years and didn't make it into a company, and a brief conversation with Dad increased my insecurity. A girl on our block turned sixteen, and her father gave her a used car. Although my own sixteenth birthday was over four years in the future, I asked Dad if he would buy me a car when I turned sixteen. He stared at me in disbelief and said, "What have you ever done for me that I would buy you a car?"

Dad wasn't the only parent who seemed eager for me to become self-supporting. Mom reminded me that the baby ballerinas of the 1930s, Irina Baronova, Tamara Toumanova, and Tatiana Riabouchinska, were as young as twelve when they began dancing with Ballet Russe. I knew I couldn't compete with the baby ballerinas. At twelve, I looked ten. With three boys to raise, Mom couldn't tour like the mothers of the baby ballerinas, and neither of my parents would co-sign a contract until I had a high school diploma. I felt that I was falling behind.

Mom also informed me that I needed to go on a diet. She said that all I had to do to lose weight was eat a little less and give up bread, so for lunch, instead of two pieces of bread with a tablespoon of peanut butter, I counted out four little Ritz crackers and put a tablespoon of peanut butter on each. There was no calorie count on the packaging, so I had no idea that I had doubled my calories, and I didn't understand why I wasn't losing weight. Like most dancers, I became obsessed with my weight.

Dancers walk a tightrope between looks and health. They have to be thin, but they also have to be strong. A dancer who is too heavy, or a dancer whose energy flags, is a dancer on unemployment. Every day, dancers work in leotards and tights in front of mirrors that show every ounce. A dancer's line is affected by weight. A dancer's jump is affected by weight. A dancer's ability to get work is affected by weight. I found ninety-two to ninety-four pounds to be a good weight for me. Below ninety-two pounds, I had too little stamina. Above ninety-four pounds, I didn't like my line; my flexibility decreased, and I had more weight to lift when I jumped. Dancers usually try to determine their peak weight and then maintain it.

In the 1970s, I knew dancers who starved themselves or threw up after meals to stay thin. At the time, many dancers considered bulimia to be a clever method of weight control. They could enjoy big meals, not get teased by bigger eaters, and still stay thin. I knew one bulimic dancer who mentioned Roman vomitoriums to give historical stature and acceptability to a less-than-elegant practice. Today, anorexia and bulimia are considered potentially fatal diseases, but in the 1950s, most people knew nothing about them. However, at age twelve, I was afraid that a diet wouldn't solve my weight problem because my muscular legs were genetic, as Mom pointed out when she said, "It's a shame you got your father's legs instead of mine."

My self-confidence continued to plummet when Mom gave me bright turquoise tights for my twelfth birthday. The last thing I wanted were tights that called attention to my thighs. I told Mom that everyone in ballet class wore pink. "Good," said Mom. "You'll stand out. Turquoise will look beautiful with your black leotard." I was stuck with turquoise tights.

I was particularly vulnerable that year because I was bored and frustrated with my classes at the Philadelphia Dance Academy. The window into the professional world that Madame Swoboda had opened was slammed shut. At the Philadelphia Dance Academy, I was placed in a small class of teenage, non-professional students, and my teacher was an American who talked like a science teacher. Instead of using metaphors and images to describe movement, she used muscle groups: "Lift your leg with the muscles beneath the leg, not the quadriceps," she said. I didn't know how to activate one muscle and deactivate another, and she couldn't explain. Instead of imagining that my fingers extended out through space, past the stars, into infinity, I imagined different muscles in my body fighting for control. When I looked in the mirror, I saw only turquoise tights that made me look like a circus performer.

The teacher told me not to force my turnout because forcing is hard on the knees, but I knew that if I didn't force my turnout, I would never acquire the necessary turnout for ballet companies. The teacher wanted me to start my pirouettes from a perfect position and would stop me mid-pirouette if one of my heels moved in advance of the rest of my body. It seemed that I was incapable of even one decent pirouette.

The Philadelphia Dance Academy also stressed the importance of learning Labanotation, a system of writing movement similar to the way music is written so that others trained in the language can read it. The system is very complex and time-consuming, and after taking a few classes, I couldn't imagine that professional dancers would have time to record dance in writing. Labanotation would have to be done by people who were not working full-time as dancers. Perhaps the school was trying to tell me that I didn't have the body or the talent to become a professional dancer. It didn't occur to me that the Preparatory Program might have been designed *not* to prepare girls for a ballet company (where girls begin careers in their teens), but to prepare them for the Undergraduate Program and careers which can begin at a later age, such as modern dance, choreography, dance criticism, dance history, and teaching.

I decided that I had to consider alternatives to ballet. I loved Perry Mason and thought I would enjoy fighting for truth and justice, but I didn't know of any female lawyers, and the Supreme Court was comprised of nine men. (It would be more than two decades before Sandra Day O'Connor became the first female Justice of the Supreme Court.)

Another career possibility was concert pianist. I had a partial scholarship to the Wilmington Music School, and I enjoyed listening to Mom's 78 rpm records of Vladimir Horowitz and Artur Rubinstein. I saw advertisements for Rudolf Serkin's concerts in the newspapers, and everybody knew the name of Van Cliburn, the 23-year-old American who had become a superstar in the spring of 1958 when he won the International Tchaikovsky Competition in Moscow. After he played, Van Cliburn received an eight-minute standing ovation, and the judges asked Premier Khrushchev if they could give first prize to an American. Khrushchev asked, "Is he the best? Then give him the prize!" Even during the Cold War, art could transcend politics. I asked my piano teacher if there were any female concert pianists. She knew of only one, Myra Hess, but no else I asked had ever heard of her, and the newspapers never mentioned female pianists. Besides, my hands were small, and I doubted I would ever be able to reach a tenth (a span of ten white keys).

Dance seemed to be my best option. It was probably the most accessible art for women because it is an art in which men and women are not interchangeable. Sleeping Beauty is always danced by a woman, and the Prince by a man, so women represent no threat to men's jobs and no man risks the indignity of seeing a woman perform his job better than he. This is not true in the other arts. On the concert stage and in symphony orchestras, instruments can be played by men or by women. In writing, painting, and architecture, the gender of the artist is not even visible in the finished work. In these arts, men could lose jobs to women if women were allowed to compete. In the 1950s, many conductors and musicians claimed that female musicians simply didn't have the strength or the temperament to play as well as men. That fallacy was later exposed when the musicians' unions began to require that auditioning musicians be hidden from the judges by screens. When this policy was first put into effect, the concert master of the Metropolitan Opera orchestra told me that the screens were pointless because the judges could hear the click of high heels as women took their places behind the screens, but women soon learned to kick off their shoes or wear flats, and when they were judged solely by the sound coming from their instruments, women came flooding into symphony orchestras—jobs previously held almost exclusively by men. But in the 1950s, many people accepted the myth that women pianists simply didn't have the digital strength to produce as good a sound as men.

Dance was also accessible to women because many of the company founders and decision-makers were female. Ninette de Valois established and ran the Royal Ballet in London; Lucia Chase was the founding patron and artistic director of Ballet Theatre in New York, and Martha Graham was the founder and director of the Martha Graham Dance Company, the best-known modern dance company in America. In the other arts, most of the decision-makers were male.

Dance was also open to women because dance is associated with grace and elegance, qualities associated with women, and like most jobs associated with women, dance had a low pay scale. Most men did not consider dance a desirable profession, so women were able to have power.

As I dragged myself to classes at the Philadelphia Dance Academy, ballet seemed to be my best prospect—even though I felt hopelessly inadequate. Then, one Sunday, I learned the difference a great teacher can make.

I had missed my Thursday afternoon class at the Philadelphia Dance Academy because of a snowstorm. Mom and I had been told that because I was in the most advanced class, I would have to make up classes I missed in a less advanced class. However, Mom and I knew that there was a Sunday class for Philadelphia Dance Academy teachers, and we suspected that this class also contained the most advanced students, which it did. This class was taught on alternate weekends by Alfredo Corvino, a teacher at the Metropolitan Opera Ballet, and James Jamieson, another New York teacher, who was reputed to be an ogre. I had heard that James Jamieson insulted students and reduced them to tears. Mom and I decided I should take my chances on Sunday and hope that Mr. Corvino was teaching, which he was.

Mr. Corvino taught the Cecchetti method, a system of dancing that is based on anatomy and is more restrained than the flamboyant Russian style of Madame Swoboda, but Mr. Corvino gave an excellent class, was encouraging to the students, and, unlike my Thursday teacher, didn't try to change the way I danced. I hoped he would be teaching the next time I had a make-up, but he wasn't. This time the teacher was the dreaded Mr. Jamieson.

I warmed up outside the classroom and looked around for a familiar face, but I didn't recognize anyone. There were several men warming up, and one of them, probably in his thirties, had a white handkerchief tied around his head. His feet, his extension, and his posture told me that he was a professional dancer, so I sneaked looks at him as he prepared for the class. He saw me looking at him and smiled—a toothy grin. A few minutes later, he walked over to me and said, "I haven't seen you here before, have I?"

I explained that I was taking a make-up class and that I'd taken the class a few weeks earlier with Mr. Corvino.

"How did you like his class?" he asked.

"I loved it," I said.

Handkerchief Man asked me where I had studied previously, and when I mentioned Madame Swoboda, he said that he knew her from New York. As he walked away, I was glad that there would be at least one friendly face in the class.

However, as I took my place at the barre, I didn't see Handkerchief Man and guessed that he was probably rehearsing in another studio. I put one leg on the barre and began to stretch. Abruptly, the buzzing in the classroom stopped. I turned to face the door, and Handkerchief Man entered the room as if he owned it. He projected more charisma than I had ever seen up close.

"First position," he said, and I realized that Handkerchief Man was the infamous James Jamieson. From the first plié (knee bend) to the last grand battement (high kick), he gave the impression that he saw every movement by every dancer in the class. He demonstrated every combination with superb Russian technique. And he did *eight* pirouettes! He was demanding, but not cruel. He made dancers want to be better, to be worthy of his time, and to live up to his high expectations.

Near the end of the class, he announced, "Sixteen fouettés to the right." I was delighted. Ever since I had seen Margot Fonteyn spin out of her fouettés in *Swan Lake*, I had been working on mine, and on that Sunday afternoon, I did them on a dime. As I looked for his response, he said, "Sixteen fouettés to the left." My heart sank. In the 1950s, few dancers could do fouettés to both sides. Like ice skaters practicing jumps, most dancers practiced these spins in only one direction. I gritted my teeth and spun to the left. As I finished the last turn, I was dizzy, but I hung onto the finish, like a gymnast who lands off balance, but manages not to do an extra bounce. When my head cleared, I realized that I was the only one who had finished all sixteen. With a smile, Mr. Jamieson looked at me and said, "Well done." I was thrilled from the tips of my toes to the top of my head.

After class, I asked Mr. Jamieson where he taught in New York, and he told me that he had opened a school in Wilmington, Delaware.

"Wilmington, Delaware!"

He invited me to his advanced class Monday through Friday at five-thirty.

Two hours earlier, I had doubted my ability to become a professional dancer. Now, I had a champion who inspired me.

A note about fouettés: these are a flashy series of spins on one leg. The supporting leg pliés (bends) while the free leg extends forward just below hip level and moves to the side. Then the free leg whips into passé (knee bent, toes pointed at the side of the knee) as the supporting leg rises on pointe for the turn. The first dancer to perform thirty-two fouettés was the Italian ballerina Pierina Legnani in the late nineteenth century. At the time, many ballet dancers labeled this tour de force a circus trick, but by the 1950s, dancers who performed the dual role of Odette/Odile in *Swan Lake* were expected to perform thirty-two fouettés, and audiences held their breath until all thirty-two were complete. Even today, some ballerinas in first-rate companies have trouble with thirty-two fouettés, but others insert doubles and even triples.

Mr. Jamieson's Academy of the Dance was housed in a charming brick building on a quiet street near the Brandywine River. The studio and the dressing rooms were on the ground floor, and the apartments of Mr. Jamieson and Helene Antonova, co-founders of the school, were on the floors above. Madame Antonova was a Russian woman in her early sixties who had danced with Ballet Russe. Her daughter, Sonia Wojcikowska, had also danced with Ballet Russe and was teaching at Carnegie Hall in New York. Madame Antonova taught the intermediate class from four-thirty to five-thirty daily. Mr. Jamieson, in his late thirties, was an internationally known Scottish dance champion who had worked with Agnes de Mille in the musicals *Oklahoma!* and *Brigadoon*. He taught the advanced class from five-thirty to seven, as well as a ballet class and a Scottish dance class on Saturdays.

When I arrived for my first class at the Academy of the Dance, Mom introduced herself to Mr. Jamieson, and Mr. Jamieson informed her that parents were not allowed to watch class. Although this policy wasn't common in Wilmington, it was standard in New York and Philadelphia, and Mom took it in stride, as she had with Madame Swoboda and the Philadelphia Dance Academy.

Banishing parents from the studio has benefits for both the children and the adults. Even when the parents don't chatter, they can be a distraction for the children. Also, when parents watch class, they may second-guess the teacher and undermine what the teacher is trying to accomplish, and when parents watch *every* class, they see good days and bad days, but when they watch at six-month intervals, they can more accurately judge the progress of their children.

Mr. Jamieson's class began with pliés (knee bends) and continued with tendus (movements of one leg from first or fifth position to a pointed foot in front, side, or back). Mr. Jamieson stared at my pointed foot:

"What's that? A dead fish?"

I arched my foot a little higher.

"Where's the perspiration? You aren't working," he said as he ran one finger across my dry forehead.

Throughout the class, he criticized everything I did. As I watched the other dancers, I realized that I was the absolute worst dancer in the class. This was a blow to my ego, but I knew that the class was exactly what I needed. I was surrounded by dancers I could emulate. Two of the girls already seemed good enough to be professionals, and even one of the weakest dancers had a fabulous extension. (She was also new to the class and eventually had a long career with the Martha Graham company.)

When Mom returned near the end of the class, Mr. Jamieson was berating me for wobbling on my grands battements (high kicks). After class, as I left the studio, Mom saw my troubled face and assumed I wouldn't want to come back.

"No," I said. "I have to come back. I'm the worst dancer in the class."

Years later, Mom told me that this was the night she knew I had the grit to become a professional dancer.

Mom told me that the people who are called "talented" are simply the ones who work the hardest, and I believed her. I hadn't yet learned that this isn't necessarily true. Some people are born with great flexibility, or a beautiful body, or an innate sense of balance, and no amount of hard work can trump these gifts. Some bodies can withstand tremendous abuse, and others break down when challenged, but when I was twelve, I believed what Mom told me: that success is the result of good training and hard work. With Mr. Jamieson, I had found the training, and no one was going to work harder than I.

When I watched TV, I sat on the floor, put the soles of my feet together, and let gravity pull my knees toward the floor. When I woke in the middle of the night, I lay on my back and stretched. Even with six dance classes a week (five ballet and one Scottish), I practiced every day. For my birthday, I asked for Saturday ballet lessons, and Mom and Dad gave me five.

With Mr. Jamieson, every class was a performance, by him and by us. He insisted that superb technique is not enough. A dancer must have stage presence. A dancer must command attention. In every class, he showed in his own performance how this is done. When a student looked at the floor, he said, "There's no money on the floor. Dance for your mother in the balcony. That's where she's sitting. It's the only seat she can afford after paying for all your dance lessons." In one class, as I danced across the room, Mr. Jamieson stopped the music in mid-combination and told me, "This is *Swan Lake*, not *Duck Pond*. Swans are elegant."

Sometimes, he'd ask about the music: "Who's the composer, and what ballet is it from?" We learned to listen to the music and then sidle up to the piano and memorize the composers' names that were printed on the sheet music.

In between the barre and the center, Mr. Jamieson and I would have pirouette contests. He'd do five. I'd do five. He'd do six. I'd do six. He'd do seven, and sometimes I'd do seven. Eight was usually enough to win, but on rare occasions, it took nine. Mr. Jamieson made it clear that audiences don't pay to see a perfect preparation. They pay to see pirouettes, and once you've got them, you can work on making them better. Mr. Jamieson was the polar opposite of my teacher at the Philadelphia Dance Academy, and I adored him.

Mr. Jamieson said, "The difference between an amateur and a professional is that a professional knows how to cheat." Dancers work on slippery stages, bumpy stages, and raked stages (stages which are higher at the back and slope toward the footlights), and professionals adapt their techniques to fit the circumstances.

In almost every class, the girls did fouettés, and the men did turns *à la seconde*. Both are a series of turns on one leg, but in fouettés, the free leg extends front, moves side, and whips into passé for the spin. In turns *à la seconde*, the free leg is extended to the side at a ninety-degree angle and remains in that position, turn after turn. Usually, the goal in both turns is to perform the spins without moving from the spot where they begin. Vic, one of the men in the class, habitually traveled to the left. One day, Mr. Jamieson placed us four feet apart with me on Vic's left. He instructed me to do fouettés and Vic to do turns *à la seconde*. In a frightening flash, I visualized my foot shattering as Vic moved into my space, but disobeying Mr. Jamieson wasn't an option. I stood tall at four feet nine inches and imagined that I had legs and feet of steel. Mr. Jamieson cued the pianist, and the music began. I did sixteen fouettés and looked to my right. Vic had just learned that he *could* spin in one spot, and I had just learned that I could perform under pressure.

On several occasions, I went upstairs to the living quarters. The first time was to meet Mr. Jamieson's father, who had come to visit. I loved talking with the older Mr. Jamieson because he had a charming Scottish accent. Another time was to have a piece of Madame Antonova's homemade cheesecake, which didn't taste at all like cake. In my experience, cake was a delivery system for frosting. This so-called cake had no frosting and tasted suspiciously like a bar of cream cheese, which was lunch, not dessert. Mr. Jamieson told me that Madame Antonova had been like a mother to him, and I wondered what had happened to his birth mother. He never mentioned her, and I wondered if she had died when he was young, because he often spoke of the respect children should have for their mothers. He also asked me about my schoolwork and emphasized the importance of getting a good education.

On one occasion, I stayed in Mr. Jamieson's and Madame Antonova's guest room. Early that afternoon, it began to snow. Mom didn't think that Mr. Jamieson would give class that night, but I suspected that he would since he lived above the school, so I asked Mom for permission to use the telephone. We had a party line (several families sharing one line), so we children were only allowed to use the telephone for a worthwhile purpose after getting Mom's permission. As I suspected, Mr. Jamieson *was* giving class that evening, but he thought it might be difficult for me to get home afterwards, so he invited me to spend the night in the guest room.

Snow continued to fall during class, and after class, the two men who were regulars, Joe and Vic, decided to go to a movie and invited me to join them. When we went outside, there were no cars in the streets, and the city looked like a winter wonderland. We walked down the middle of the street, and I felt an amazing freedom as I broke the everyday rules. As if in a movie, I bounded down the street in a series of grands jetés (big jumps from one foot to the other). When I looked back at Joe and Vic, they were doing a bouncy walking step.

"What's that?" I asked.

"Don't you know?" said Joe.

"No," I said.

"It's from *The Wizard of Oz*. It's the step on the yellow brick road."

Joe and Vic taught me the step, and the three of us danced down Market Street, like Dorothy and two of her friends.

That night, the movie we saw was *Village of the Damned*. The story takes place in a town in which all of the women mysteriously become pregnant and give birth to alien children with big eyes and blond hair. The movie was terrifying and reminded me of a pregnancy fear that had been equally terrifying when I was younger. One Christmas Eve, as the minister told the story of Mary and Joseph and the inn with no room, a disturbing thought entered my mind: what if God chose me to be the virgin for the Second Coming? What if I had to be the Virgin Lee? I didn't want the responsibility for raising Jesus and I didn't want my stomach blowing up like a balloon; on the other hand, I couldn't thwart God's will or He'd turn me into a pillar of salt. What were the odds of becoming the Virgin Lee? I did the math: if I got with child immediately after college, my son would be thirty-three at the millennium. These were terrible odds. I decided I might have to become a nun. If I were a nun, God probably wouldn't get me pregnant because he wouldn't want a scandal in His church. As a nun, I could be safe.

By the time I saw *Village of the Damned*, I was pretty sure that God knew that I was in no way qualified to raise His son, but that fear had been replaced by another. In the newspapers, there were photographs of babies with flippers for arms because their mothers had been given the drug thalidomide for morning sickness. As I watched the movie with the alien babies, I was glad that I was going to be a ballerina. Ordinary women were expected to have children, and if they didn't, other women whispered about the tragedy of the barren woman, and they congratulated themselves on their own fecundity. However, *ballerinas* who didn't have children—ballerinas like Margot Fonteyn—were considered disciplined and ethereal. After all, no one wants to see a pregnant Swan Queen wobbling around on pointe. I was glad that I was going to become a ballerina and wouldn't even have to *think* about children until I was ancient and retired—at least thirty or thirty-five.

As Joe and Vic walked me back to Mr. Jamieson's after the movie, I reveled in our defiance of time. Usually I had to be in bed at nine o'clock, but not tonight. Tonight I was among dancers, and dancers live by a different clock. Most of the city was asleep, but we dancers didn't have to get up at seven to rush to the office. We could enjoy the moon shining on the snow and the stars twinkling so much brighter now that the windows of the buildings were dark. We weren't barraged by the honking horns of the garish day. We could see things and feel things that the rest of the world was too busy to see.

Dancers live by a different time clock—both time of day and time of life. Dancers are night people. They begin their workday between 9:00 AM and 11:00 AM with company class, and although they rehearse all day, they must be at peak performance between 8:00 PM and 11:00 PM. After the performance, they have dinner. In New York, the Broadway bowling league is in full swing around midnight, a time when most "civilians" are home in bed.

Dancers also see time of life (life stages) differently from most people. Dancers often commit to their careers by the time they are ten. By their early teens, they are auditioning for summer programs and trying to determine their viability in the marketplace. When other young men and women are choosing a college, dancers are looking for jobs. And in their thirties and forties, when most other people are established in their careers, dancers are beginning a new one. Some become dance teachers or choreographers, but many go to college and train for new careers alongside people half their age.

Mr. Jamieson was a champion Scottish dancer and insisted that I take his Scottish dance classes every Saturday as his guest. He taught both the country dances and the five competition dances: the Highland Fling, the

Sword Dance, the Sean Truibhas, the Irish Jig, and the Sailors' Hornpipe. The country dances are performed by groups of dancers; the competition dances are performed by individuals.

The Highland Fling is the quintessential Scottish dance and is performed with pride, even arrogance. The Sword Dance is performed around a sword and scabbard which the dancer places in the pattern of a cross. The dancer must dance as close to the sword as possible without touching it. If the sword moves, the dancer is eliminated. The Sean Truibhas is the most balletic dance and has steps that skim the ground like a pebble bouncing across a lake. The Irish Jig is an exuberant tap dance in shoes with no taps. Finally, the Sailors' Hornpipe is a character piece in which the feet do intricate steps while the arms pull on imaginary ropes. When Mr. Jamieson performed the Scottish dances, his upper body looked as if he were posing for Rodin while his feet cut through the air like knives. His jumps were as effortless as a bouncing ball. During the three years I studied with him, I don't recall ever seeing him look tired, bored, or ill.

There are some technical differences between Scottish dance and ballet. In ballet, dancers leap and land so that their heels usually touch the floor between movements. In Scottish dance, dancers rise on demi-pointe (on the balls of their feet) at the beginning of the dance, and their heels don't touch the floor until the end. In ballet, the passé position has a foot pointed at the knee, but in Scottish dance, as the pointed foot reaches the supporting leg, it flexes slightly so that the free foot is placed with the heel under the knee and the foot exactly parallel to and hugging the supporting leg. In ballet, when a dancer raises her arms above her head in high fifth, her arms form a circle around her head with the middle fingers pointing at each other, only inches apart. In Scottish dance, the arms are wider apart and the middle fingers lightly touch the opposing thumbs.

Mr. Jamieson and Madame Antonova took me to my first Scottish games, which are a combination of picnic, music competition, athletic competition, and dance competition, and are attended by people of Scottish descent from all over the world. As we approached the site of the games, we heard the sound of bagpipes, and the music continued non-stop throughout the day with band competitions, individual competitions, and accompaniment for the dance competitions. The athletic events included caber throwing, Scottish hammer, and putting of the stone. Mr. Jamieson explained all of the events, and we watched them for several minutes, but we were both eager to get to the dance stage.

The dance competition was divided into age groups with Eight and Under as the youngest, and Fifteen and Older as the oldest. During the competition, Mr. Jamieson explained to me what the judges were looking for and why particular dancers won. Winners in the younger groups received medals; winners in the oldest group received small cash prizes.

I could see that Mr. Jamieson was loved and respected by many of the dancers who were competing in the games, and as Mr. Jamieson introduced me, I knew that when I began competing, I would be representing him as well as myself. But as I watched and listened, I realized that Mr. Jamieson was a champion, and whether I won or lost, he would remain a champion. I was his student and his protégée, but he would have many more. Mr. Jamieson didn't need me to validate his life. He was like a cyclist who takes the lead and allows the rider behind him to benefit from his back draft. At some point, when I was older, I would have to ride out from behind him and forge my own path, but for the time being, I was the beneficiary of his talent, hard work, and generosity.

The summer I was thirteen, Mr. Jamieson decided that I was ready to compete, and he found me a Buchanan kilt that another girl in the area had outgrown. That summer and the next, Mom drove me to Scottish games throughout the northeastern part of the United States. My biggest competition in many of the games came from twin girls from Toronto who wore identical purple plaid kilts. I never knew how the judges could choose between them, but their mother told me that one twin regularly placed higher in one dance and the other twin in another. The games usually took place outdoors, and my wool jacket and wool socks were hot in the blazing sun. I took off the jacket between dances, but I never let it out of my sight because we all had to be ready to dance at a moment's notice. Different age groups were scheduled for different starting times, but the exact schedule depended on how many dancers were entered and how long it took the judges to fill out their scorecards.

The judges graded us on technique, musicality, artistic interpretation, and deportment (personal appearance). Before each of the three Scottish dances, I made sure that the shoelaces of my traditional ghillies were knotted and tucked in, that my flashes (garters) were perfectly aligned, and that my skirt fell just above the center of my kneecap. On hot days, it was a relief to get out of the kilt into the lightweight, more comfortable costumes for the Irish Jig and the Sailors' Hornpipe.

During the summers of 1959 and 1960, I won gold, silver, and bronze medals, and in one competition in which the oldest category was Fourteen and Older, I won several dollars in cash. I loved competing, and I learned valuable skills. I learned to dance in less than optimal conditions. Sometimes it was hot; other times it was windy. Sometimes there was a rickety stage, and sometimes a judge was distracted. I learned to take those things in stride and do the best I could with the circumstances I was given. I learned to carry a book to every competition so that I wouldn't burn up energy socializing between dances. I also learned to eat small snacks throughout the day so that I would be ready to perform at a moment's notice. In scheduled performances, dancers know roughly what time they will go on, but in rehearsals, they don't—especially in technical rehearsals when problems with sets or costumes can upend the schedule. In television and film, dancers work six-hour stretches between meals and may be called at any moment to produce work that will haunt them forever if it isn't good. I found that doing a few dance steps every ten or fifteen minutes and snacking periodically would allow me to spring into action at a moment's notice. Years later, when I was performing in the Broadway show *Meet Me in St. Louis*, a girl entered the dressing room and asked, "Which dressing table is Lee's?" A chorus of voices responded: "The one with the food!"

Mr. Jamieson's passion for dance reawakened and magnified my own. He gave me a solid Russian technique and showed me the importance of commanding the attention of the audience. He taught me to focus on the important matters first and worry about the details later. He taught me that each generation of dancers has an obligation to share its knowledge with the next generation. And he gave me back my confidence. For the three years I studied with Mr. Jamieson, I assumed that when I finished high school, he would guide me into a professional career. I never suspected that when I was fifteen, Mom would cut him out of my life.

4   Academic Hurdles,

1959–1961

One spring morning, a school official knocked on our door and said he had received a formal complaint that Mom had not registered her children for school. Mom explained that she was homeschooling her children, but Mom didn't have a teaching credential, so the man ordered her to send all school-age children to school the following morning. At the time, I was old enough for seventh grade, Trick for sixth, and Twink for second, so the three of us had to report to school. Tuck was only five, so he could stay home.

Mom had a very low opinion of public education. She had attended public school and said she was bored until graduate school. When she was in college, her father required her to take enough education courses to get a teaching credential in case she ever wanted or needed to teach, and Mom said that all of the education courses were a complete waste of time. She was particularly critical of the public school policy of social promotion. When Mom started school in the late 1920s, children had to pass examinations to progress from one grade to the next; if they didn't pass, they were held back and given a second chance to learn the material. By the 1950s, educators had decided that children should be promoted whether or not they could do the work because flunking children damaged their self-esteem. Mom's retort: "Let's see how much self-esteem they'll have when they graduate from high school and can't get a job because they can't read." She also thought schools were allocating too much time and money to raising the level of the below-average students to almost-average instead of identifying and shaping the gifted students who would one day lead the country. She predicted that with social promotion and the focus on the less-gifted children, it would take only one or two generations before Americans had plenty of self-esteem but were deficient in math and science. (In fact, according to the documentary *Waiting for Superman*, the 2003 PISA tests indicated that out of thirty developed countries, U.S. students ranked twenty-fifth in math, twenty-first in science, and first in confidence.)

The day after the school official knocked on our door, Trick, Twink, and I walked to the nearest public school where a man told us that we had to take IQ and achievement tests before we were assigned to classes. He said that we had to take the tests in three different classrooms so that we couldn't cheat. I was insulted. At home, we worked on the honor system, and in all of the dance classes I had ever taken, the teachers respected the students, and the students respected the teachers. The issue of cheating didn't arise.

In dance, cheating in the academic sense of the word is impossible. Everyone in the class can see the proficiency of everyone else. No dancer can claim another dancer's turnout or pirouettes as her own. In dance, "cheating" has an entirely different meaning. Dancers cheat a double tour en l'air (two revolutions in the air) when they fail to complete both revolutions in the air, but begin or end the jump with an extra hop or do part of the revolution on the floor. (This cheat is similar to under-rotation in skating.) Dancers can also cheat a preparation by moving out of a classical position into a less-perfect position. These cheats can be seen by anyone who is watching. Cheats can be a way to achieve additional revolutions, can be the effect of inattention or exhaustion, or can be a conscious choice by dancers to give themselves better stability or torque for the following movement.

At the end of our first school day, another official knocked on the door and informed Mom that Twink had cheated on his IQ test. Mom burst out laughing. The official launched into a lecture about cheating, and Mom snapped back: "My children don't cheat." The official said that a psychologist would give Twink an oral examination that precluded cheating. "You do that," said Mom. "Then we'll talk." As she closed the door, she shook her head in disbelief and said, "It hasn't even occurred to them that if a seven-year-old can figure out how to cheat on an IQ test, he's probably pretty darn smart."

Twink was vindicated by the oral exam, but no one at the school apologized. Public school was living down to Mom's expectations, and the worst was yet to come.

Dad got a copy of the Delaware law, which stated that all children had to go to school unless the superintendent of the school district stipulated that they were getting an adequate elementary school education. Dad believed that the superintendent would have to rule in our favor because our achievement tests were several grades ahead of our ages, and with very little time to prepare, we had sailed through final exams in classes ahead of our age levels. Unfortunately, the superintendent wasn't given a chance to rule. The school board decided that an elementary school education covered only the first six grades, so Twink could stay home, but Trick and I had to go to school. Mom was furious that "so-called educators" were fighting to give her children an inferior education to improve the ranking of their school. Dad consulted a lawyer who said that when the law was passed, an elementary school education was the only required education, so he thought we could win in court, but the battle would be long and expensive. After a family meeting, it was agreed that Trick and I should go to private school.

Mom took Trick and me to Tower Hill, one of the most prestigious, most expensive private schools in Wilmington, where, after another battery of tests, Trick and I were accepted into the eighth and ninth grades. However, as we read the Tower Hill handbook, we discovered that Tower Hill had compulsory athletics from 3:00 PM to 5:00 PM. The school refused to waive the requirement for me even though I had an athletic ballet class every evening. At Tower Hill, I would have to go directly from athletics to ballet class. When I got home at seven-thirty, I would have only two hours to eat dinner, practice the piano, do my homework, and take my bath. The schedule was impossible, so Mom took me to visit Tatnall, a small private girls' school where the school day ended at two-thirty, and the only compulsory athletics were gym classes twice a week during school hours.

The headmaster of the upper school, Mr. Firth, was British, formal, and friendly, and I liked him the minute we met. He asked me about my favorite subject, and when I said it was math, he told me that Tatnall had just hired a new algebra teacher, Dr. Conwell, who had been teaching boys at Yale. I was glad to hear that a girls' school was strong in math because math was generally considered to be a boys' subject. (As recently as 1992, twenty years after Title IX prohibited sex discrimination in educational institutions receiving government funds, the popular Talking Barbie doll was programmed to tell girls, "math class is tough.")

Mom stayed in the school's forum while Mr. Firth and I toured the grounds. There were athletic fields for lacrosse and other sports and four swimming pools for families to enjoy during the summer. There were no locks on the students' lockers because Tatnall, like Tower Hill, ran on the honor system—a more comfortable environment for me than the suspicious, accusatory environment of the public school. I told Mr. Firth that I was planning to become a professional ballet dancer, but that I also wanted to get a first-rate high school education. Mr. Firth assured me that I could pursue both goals at Tatnall.

My biggest concern was that school was so time-consuming. At home, I could finish my schoolwork in a few hours. At Tatnall, I would have to spend six hours a day in school and would still have homework in the evening. With homeschooling, I could sleep until I woke. For Tatnall, I'd have to be in the car at seven-fifteen so that Dad could drop off Trick at Tower Hill and me at Tatnall before he went to work at eight. For the first time in my life, I wouldn't get an optimal amount of sleep.

Nevertheless, I loved everything about Tatnall—the girls, the teachers, the curriculum, and a hundred acres of trees that turned gold, orange, and red during the fall. The teachers at Tatnall knew that I wanted to become a professional ballet dancer, and most of them supported my goal, but I was a guest in a world that wasn't mine. I was the new girl, the youngest girl, the shortest girl, and the only girl who expected to earn a living at the age of seventeen. Most of my twenty-one classmates would probably go to Seven Sisters schools, marry Ivy League husbands, and live the upper class version of Mom's life—a life I didn't want.

My recognition of my outsider status at school was concurrent with my feeling more and more like an insider in the world of dance. Mr. Jamieson introduced me to live musical theatre when he took me to see a production of *Oklahoma!* which he directed and choreographed. I already knew the opening song, "Oh, What a Beautiful Morning," because Dad sang it whenever he mowed the lawn, and I loved seeing the entire show on stage. On weekends, I listened to the Broadway cast albums of *My Fair Lady, Gigi,* and *West Side Story* and memorized all the lyrics. I wasn't alone in loving cast albums. In the 1950s, they often went to the top of the charts.

Mr. Jamieson and Madame Antonova took me to see Ballet Russe, and after the performance, they escorted me backstage and introduced me to ballerina Nora Kaye, who gave me an autograph. That night I could never have imagined that over twenty years later, I would work with Nora Kaye in the movie *Pennies from Heaven* in which I was one of more than one hundred tap dancers and she was a producer.

Mr. Jamieson and Madame Antonova allowed me to practice the piano at their studio five days a week before Madame Antonova's Intermediate Ballet class at four-thirty. On several occasions when the pianist was late, I played for the four-thirty class and learned that accompanying dance is an art. The pianist has to choose music that enhances the choreography and then must play the music at the speed and with the style that the teacher and the dancers require, which can vary from group to group within a class.

Mr. Jamieson also gave me a variety of performing experiences. With several other students, I performed Scottish dances in theatres in Philadelphia, PA, and Nyack, New York. I did a skeleton dance with cartwheels for a Halloween party. And partnered by Mr. Jamieson, I performed the lead in my first real ballet, *Fifth Symphony*, to music by Tchaikovsky—a performance we repeated for WFIL TV's *Exploring the Fine Arts.*

At WFIL, I learned that dancing on television is very different from performing on stage because unlike a live audience, the camera can move and give different perspectives on the action. When Mr. Jamieson and I arrived at the television studio, I located the cameraman, showed him a few fouettés, and asked him not to move the camera during these turns because I would be spotting the camera. (When dancers spot, they look at one spot during the first half of a turn and then whip their heads around to focus on the same spot for the second half of the turn. This is something all classical dancers do, but ice skaters do not, because skaters spin too fast.) However, during the live broadcast, I realized that the camera was drifting to my right. Alarm bells went off in my head. If I continued to spot the camera, my sense of "front" would be wherever the camera went, and I would lose my sense of direction. This was why Mr. Jamieson had told me that professionals have to adapt. As I continued to spin, I let the camera move out of my sightline and spotted a void. My fouettés ended dead front as planned. Mr. Jamieson had prepared me well.

The one teacher at Tatnall who didn't approve of my career choice was my guidance counselor, Latin teacher, and home room teacher, Mrs. Oviatt, who told me that my becoming a dancer was "a waste of a very good mind." She was the first person, but not the last, to tell me that dancers don't have to be smart, but in my experience, most world-class dancers are smart, wellread, well-traveled, and often speak several languages. In the twenty-first century, when many adults are going back to college, dancers are finding second careers as doctors, lawyers, and college professors, and the skills they learned as dancers—discipline, hard work, and passion for their jobs—follow them into their new careers.

In January of my sophomore year at Tatnall, Mrs. Oviatt decided that her second-year Latin class wasn't enough of a challenge, and despite my objection that I didn't have time for additional schoolwork, Mrs. Oviatt formed an accelerated class for me and one other girl. She couldn't have done this at a worse time because in the evenings, after my ballet class, I was rehearsing *Annie Get Your Gun*, a musical based on the life of sharpshooter Annie Oakley, which Mr. Jamieson was directing and choreographing. Rehearsing the show was the most exciting experience of my fifteen years. I was enthralled by Annie's song "They Say That Falling in Love is Wonderful," and

I loved the fact that Annie could out-shoot and out-sing the male lead, the rival sharpshooter, Frank Butler. I wrote out the lyrics of the songs and hid them inside my textbooks. Unfortunately, while the other girl in my Latin class was translating *Gallia est omnis divisa*, Mrs. Oviatt caught me memorizing the lyrics to the delightful song "I've Got the Sun in the Morning," and told me that my outside activities were becoming an unhealthy obsession. I explained my priorities: dance first, piano second, school third.

"School should be first," she said.

"Not if I'm going to become a professional dancer," I said.

Mrs. Oviatt related this conversation to my parents and Mr. Firth at the next parent/teacher meeting. As she looked to Mr. Firth for support, he said, "I have to agree with Lee."

Little did Mrs. Oviatt know that the other shoe was about to drop.

The preceding spring, Mr. Jamieson had taken me to company class with Ballet Russe while the company was performing in Wilmington. When we arrived at the DuPont Playhouse, Mr. Jamieson introduced me to the ballet mistress, and while he and she chatted about Madame Antonova and the other people they both knew, I watched the company dancers trickle into the studio. The dancers hugged and kissed each other hello and conversed in several different languages. They had the relaxed camaraderie that comes when a company works together, travels together, eats together, and sleeps in the same hotels.

During the class, I particularly enjoyed watching the men—especially in the big jump combinations. At Mr. Jamieson's, we had two or three men in class, but here, there were many more. For me, the class was a performance. For the company dancers, class was the beginning of a dance-filled day that would culminate in the evening performance. I could hardly wait to become a member of this glamorous, multicultural, closely knit community.

On the way home, Mr. Jamieson told me that after the class, the ballet mistress had told him that if I had been sixteen, she would have taken me into the company on the spot. I relayed this information to Mom, whose face clouded over as if a giant storm had moved in.

"That's good, isn't it?" I asked.

"In the *corps!*" said Mom scornfully. "Is that where you want to be? In the *corps*?!"

I could think of nothing more wonderful than being in the corps de ballet of Ballet Russe where I could watch world-class dancers every day, but I answered Mom as she demanded, "Of course not. But I'll be a lot better in two years."

"You'd better be," said Mom. And she walked away.

Mom's desperation caught me by surprise, but it shouldn't have. Mom was a smart, well-educated woman trapped in an increasingly unhappy marriage in a society that expected her to spend her adult life as an unpaid cook, maid, nanny, and sexual partner for her husband. Divorce carried a terrible stigma. I knew of only one girl at Tatnall whose parents were divorced, and people whispered the word "divorced" the way they whispered the word "cancer," as if saying it out loud made it contagious. Some women in Mom's position spent their days shopping for avocado appliances while others dulled the pain with afternoon cocktails, but Mom poured all of her energy and ambition into her children.

Although Mom was disappointed with me that spring, the company class with Ballet Russe had established two things: that I was ballet company material and that my sixteenth birthday was the earliest I could expect to get a job.

Nine months later, during my sophomore year at Tatnall, Mom made her move. She informed me that she had asked Tatnall to let me skip eleventh grade, and Tatnall had refused, so she had signed me up for college boards. Her goal was to catapult me from tenth grade into college. Instead of two more years of high school, she wanted me to spend the fall semester in college and then join a ballet company on my sixteenth birthday, which conveniently fell in January, at the end of the fall semester. Mom told me not to discuss this plan with Dad (she would be the intermediary) or to breathe a word about college boards to anyone outside the family. She didn't want Mrs. Oviatt to find out what we were doing and cancel the exams.

That March, in addition to my regular schedule of nine subjects at school, piano practice at Mr. Jamieson's, ballet classes, homework, and performances of *Annie Get Your Gun*, Mom had added college boards. I had two recurring dreams. In the first, I was being chased by a herd of buffalo. I ran as fast as I could, but when I looked back, I could see that the buffalo were gaining. When I looked forward again, there was a precipice. I screeched to a stop, but before I could figure out what to do, the buffalo jumped on my back. Every night I woke up gasping for breath, with my back arched high against the covers. In the other dream, I was a spirit hovering above the back left fender of our light green Plymouth station wagon, which was parked in our driveway. I was watching a faceless man in a cap who was standing in our front yard looking at the front door. I knew that the man had killed me and Mom and Dad, but I didn't know why, and I didn't know whether or not he was justified. As I watched him, I knew that my job was to protect my brothers inside the house, but being a spirit was new to me, and I had no idea how I was going to do this. As the man walked toward the front door of our house, I woke up. It doesn't take a genius to know how I felt about the race toward my career or about leaving my family for a new world. The dreams were disturbing my sleep, so I took action. Every night as I climbed into bed, I closed my eyes and visualized a vertical, brightly lit tic-tac-toe board, like the board on a television game show. In each square was a category: baseball, ballet, ancient Greece, *Annie Get Your Gun*, et cetera. As I drifted off to sleep, I chose a category and dreamed about that. If my dreams strayed off the chosen subject, the rules demanded that the board reappear so that I could choose another subject. In retrospect, I am astonished that this idea worked, but it did.

The college boards were held at Trick's school, Tower Hill. I sat in the middle of the front row, followed the instructions of the monitor, and took five examinations. I told myself that if I did poorly, no one would know except Mom and me. Boy, was I wrong! When I arrived at school on Monday, Mrs. Oviatt was waiting for me, and she was using her accusatory voice:

"You took the college boards!" she said.

"How did you know?" I asked.

"My husband was the monitor," she said. "When he came home Saturday afternoon, he told me that there was a baby in the front row. I asked him if the baby had a bow on her ponytail, and he said, 'Yes, she did.'"

Mrs. Oviatt was particularly upset that I had taken three achievement tests. "You're in the tenth grade," she said. "You haven't even taken the courses that these examinations test. You'll embarrass the school."

I admitted that I hadn't had time to finish the English composition exam, but Mom had told me to take five exams, and so I had. Relations were tense between Mrs. Oviatt and me until one morning when she flew across the forum and hugged me.

"You got a 722 in English composition!" she said.

I was annoyed with myself for not keeping an eye on the clock. English composition was the only exam on which I had any chance of scoring a perfect 800. However, Mom said that the combination of my test scores and my dance ability should be enough to get me into whatever college we chose, and that was all that mattered.

I had mixed feelings about Mom's accelerated plan. Part of me hoped that I wouldn't get into college so that I could spend two more years at Tatnall and continue to study and perform with Mr. Jamieson. I had been looking forward to English history in the eleventh grade because I was fascinated by the machinations of the English kings and queens. I wanted to perform in more musicals with Mr. Jamieson because I enjoyed the singing and the acting as much as the dancing. I wanted a high school diploma—not just a few months of college. I wanted to get used to my new body, which had grown four inches and developed curves. I wanted more time before I had to prove myself. But I knew I didn't have it. Mom was pushing me out of the nest.

The next Saturday morning, when Dad took the boys to the YMCA, Mom and I kicked off our shoes, sat on the sofa, and plotted my early escape from the suburbs. The first college Mom proposed was Bennington in Vermont. One of the dancers from Mr. Jamieson's was attending Bennington and loved the school. It was highly rated in both academics and dance. However, the names of the dancers associated with Bennington, which included Martha Graham, José Limón, and Hanya Holm, read like a *Who's Who* of modern dance, not ballet. I didn't want to learn a new dance form at this late date—especially one that was *not* based on turnout and was performed in bare feet. I had only a few months before I would be expected to embark on a career in toe shoes and tutus.

I told Mom that I wanted to go to college in New York so that I could study at one of the ballet company schools: the Ballet Russe School, the School of American Ballet, or the Ballet Theatre School.

Mom found three colleges in New York: Sarah Lawrence, Barnard, and Juilliard. Sarah Lawrence, like Bennington, was a girls' school with high academic standards and a strong dance department. Like Bennington, it specialized in modern dance. Sarah Lawrence had an independent spirit that Mom thought I would like, but it was located in Bronxville, not Manhattan, so I placed it third on my list. Barnard was the sister school to Columbia University, had strong academic standards, and was only a short subway ride from the ballet company schools, so I placed it second. My first choice was Juilliard because it was one of the best music schools in the country, and I liked the idea of getting credit for my piano practice. Like Barnard, it was a short subway ride from the company schools. As I read about Juilliard, I discovered that the college also had a dance department, and that I had already met one of the teachers, Alfredo Corvino, whose class I had taken at the Philadelphia Dance Academy. The other ballet teachers were Margaret Craske and Antony Tudor. All three teachers were also on the faculty of the Metropolitan Opera Ballet School. If Juilliard accepted me as a dance major, I might be able to glide seamlessly from one semester of college into the Metropolitan Opera Ballet or even into Ballet Theatre, where Antony Tudor had choreographed *Pillar of Fire* and *Romeo and Juliet*. Antony Tudor was a busy choreographer, so I guessed that the primary ballet teachers at Juilliard would be Alfredo Corvino, who taught the Cecchetti method, and Margaret Craske, whose style I didn't know. Mom and I decided to drive to New York to see Margaret Craske and then visit the School of American Ballet, which was the most publicized ballet school in New York and which had been co-founded by the Russian-trained George Balanchine.

5 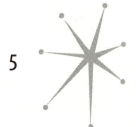 Falling in Love with New York, Spring 1961

During spring break, Mom and I drove to New York in our new white Plymouth station wagon with futuristic fins. As we drove into the city, I saw the New York skyline for the first time, and it took my breath away. I was awed by the skyscrapers shooting into the sky. Each building had thousands of windows with thousands of people behind them, like bees in a beehive, and all these people had different stories, different lives, and different dreams.

As we entered midtown Manhattan, I was thrilled by the sight of dozens of theatres, one after the next, running north and south, east and west. Some were big theatres like the Metropolitan Opera House and City Center. Others were mid-sized theatres for Broadway shows, and others were small theatres for cabaret. Five years earlier, when I began taking the train to Philadelphia, I had memorized the names of the theatres, the plays, and the stars that I saw on three sheets, the vertical posters in train stations that advertised Broadway shows. Now I was seeing the actual theatres, and inside the theatres were the biggest stars on Broadway: Mary Martin, Chita Rivera, Gwen Verdon, and Diahann Carroll. I could feel the heartbeat of the professional world, and I liked its quicker pace.

In midtown Manhattan, Mom and I found the Metropolitan Opera Ballet School, which was located in the Metropolitan Opera House, a grand old building that occupied an entire block from Thirty-Eighth Street to Thirty-Ninth Street, from Seventh Avenue to Broadway. The stage door was on Thirty-Ninth Street, and as Mom and I entered, I could feel the ghosts of the great singers and dancers who had performed in the theatre, whose souls were still there because they couldn't bear to leave. The doorman was a friendly old man, straight out of Central Casting, and there was an old elevator that ran with a lever that moved like a windshield wiper, from left to right. The further right it went, the faster the speed of the elevator. The elevator lumbered up to the top floor, where there was a large dance studio overlooking the city. The studio, like the rest of the theatre, reverberated with history. I felt as if I had walked into a Degas painting, and I luxuriated in the feeling of stepping back in time.

Mrs. Craske was teaching class, but, as a teacher for me, she had two strikes against her. First, she had a gentle, nurturing personality rather than a theatrical presence like Mr. Jamieson, and I preferred the more theatrical personality. Second, she taught the Cecchetti method, not Russian technique. But before Mom and I left the building, I asked the doorman to let me look at the stage.

The Metropolitan Opera House had the biggest stage I had ever seen. I couldn't imagine how many grand jetés it would take to get from one side of the stage to the other. Or how many miles it was from the stage floor to the ceiling. From the edge of the wings, I walked center stage, a distance of more than fifty feet, and looked out into the maroon and gold Edwardian auditorium that was shaped like a golden horseshoe on five levels. Hanging from the ceiling, high above the five levels of seats, was a sunburst chandelier. The auditorium seated over three thousand people, and almost a quarter of the seats were in elegant boxes with room to move the chairs around for a better view. I knew that kings and queens, movie stars and captains of industry sat in those seats, and I vowed that someday I would dance on this stage and hear the applause of those three thousand people. My trip to the Metropolitan Opera would have been worth it just to walk onto the stage.

Mom and I had dinner at the Automat, which I adored. Opposite the entrance was a cafeteria line with salads, meats, potatoes, and vegetables. I loved being able to choose exactly what I wanted—mashed potatoes and green beans. On the two side walls were cubbyholes with glass fronts. Inside the cubbyholes were rolls, pastries, and pies. I put a few nickels in the slot by one cubbyhole, lifted the glass panel, and took out a slice of lemon meringue pie, which was immediately replaced with another slice by a hand on the other side of the cubbyhole. Built into the walls were metal machines that dispensed coffee and hot chocolate. I watched a man place a cup under a faucet, insert two nickels into a slot, and swivel a metal lever. Coffee poured out of the faucet into the cup just until the cup was full. There were separate machines for black coffee, regular coffee, light coffee, and hot chocolate, so people didn't even have to add milk.

In contrast to the Metropolitan Opera House, which pulsed with history, the atmosphere at the School of American Ballet was one of cool efficiency. I took two classes at SAB and preferred the class of Anatole Oboukhoff, a short man with a large presence. Mr. Oboukhoff gave a good class, and I could see that the girls would be excellent competition, but Mr. Oboukhoff didn't seem to find much joy in the performance of his students. I didn't think I would look forward to seeing him the way I looked forward to seeing Mr. Jamieson, and I had learned at the Philadelphia Dance Academy how important it was to find a teacher who inspired me.

That night, as Mom and I drove back to Wilmington, I concluded that our trip had been productive. I hadn't found my inspirational teacher, but I had fallen in love with New York. I could see myself living and dancing in this magical city. New York had all of the energy and diversity of the dancers I saw on stage and television. I loved seeing people from many different cultures, like the Orthodox Jews in the diamond district and the French, Chinese, and Greeks in ethnic restaurants. I liked hearing many different languages in the streets. I was dazzled by the bright lights of Broadway, and I knew I wanted to live in a city that pulses with life twenty-four hours a day.

It may seem strange that we were only a few miles from Juilliard (which was then on 122nd Street) and never went to see the campus, but I wasn't looking for a campus. I had seen what I needed to see when I watched the class with Mrs. Craske. I had learned that I wanted to be a piano major at Juilliard and study ballet at a company school.

Piano recitals and competitions indicated that I might be the best pianist my age in Delaware, but Delaware was a small state, and I knew that only a few miles away, across the Pennsylvania state line, was Peter Serkin, the son of concert pianist Rudolf Serkin. I hadn't heard Peter play, but I had heard that he was following in his father's footsteps. I was sure that he practiced more than one hour a day and that his hands, unlike mine, would be big enough to reach a tenth. My competition for Juilliard would be pianists like him, not part-time pianists like me. Mom and I decided that I should take the dance audition at Juilliard as a backup.

When we drove back into Wilmington after two days in New York, the fourteen-story DuPont buildings looked puny compared to the skyscrapers of Manhattan. Wilmington seemed like a sleepy little hamlet of detached houses and picket fences. It had been a great place to grow up. Wilmington had given me nurturing teachers and scholarships for music, dance, and high school, but now I felt ready to be part of a bigger world.

That night, Mom and I filled out the application for Juilliard. We never discussed the possibility that Juilliard wouldn't want me, so by the end of April, I believed that I was poised to make my escape from the suburbs. In fact, our search for academic and ballet schools had just begun.

Juilliard had specific requirements for the piano audition: a work by Bach; a complete sonata by Haydn, Mozart, or Beethoven; a Romantic piece by Chopin, Mendelssohn, Schumann, Brahms, or Liszt; and a piece by a twentieth-century composer. My piano teacher, Miss Littell, decided what I would play. In all the years I studied piano, it never occurred to me to suggest a particular piece or even a particular composer. In piano, as in dance, my teacher spoke, and I obeyed.

For my Juilliard audition, Miss Littell chose a Bach prelude and fugue in C minor, which I thought was repetitive and bland; Beethoven's Sonata,

Opus 2, No. 2, which I liked because it began with a bang and had several different moods within its four movements; a piece by Chopin called "Three Ecossaises," which was my favorite because it required speed and dexterity so that the notes sparkled like musical diamonds; and Aaron Copland's "The Cat and the Mouse," a modern piece which I actively disliked. Even the name of the Copland piece offended me because it sounded like the title of a nursery rhyme. This was the first modern piece I had ever played, and I tried to convince Miss Littell to find a twentieth-century composer who wrote in the Romantic style, but she was adamant that Juilliard required a twentieth-century piece because the jury wanted to hear something modern. I didn't appreciate modern music or modern dance. I didn't like dissonance, and I didn't like anguished contractions. My sensibility was firmly rooted in the Romantic era. I liked the music of Beethoven, Brahms, Chopin, Tchaikovsky, Liszt, Schumann, and Schubert. I liked the Romantic ballets: *Giselle, Swan Lake, Coppélia*, and *Sleeping Beauty*.

As a dress rehearsal for my piano audition, Mom decided that I should give a recital at the Wilmington Music School on May 30th—two days before my auditions at Juilliard. I was surprised by the large audience, pleased that no one left at intermission, and satisfied with the way I played. Even "The Cat and the Mouse" was tolerable because the audience seemed to enjoy it. However, the most important thing I learned from the recital was that I didn't have the temperament of a concert pianist. I didn't like spending hours alone practicing the piano, and I didn't enjoy the solo concert as much as I enjoyed dance performances in which I was part of a group.

Dancers spend their days leaping and spinning in the company of other dancers. Every morning in the dressing room, they share their hopes, fears, and dreams as they change into practice clothes for company class. They take class together, rehearse together, and perform together. Even a dancer who is rehearsing a solo usually has at least two other people in the room— the choreographer or ballet mistress and the accompanist. Professional ballet dancers are part of a large community. The company is their immediate family, and their community circles the globe. It is a community that lives in studios with mirrors on one wall, communicates in French, strives for perfection, and inspires other members with passion for the art. I liked the physical feeling of dance and the exhilaration of conquering new steps and performing on stage, but part of my love for dance was a love of the community.

This revelation about my unsuitability for a career as a pianist didn't change my desire to be a piano major at Juilliard because Juilliard excelled in piano, and I wanted to study ballet at a company school with Russian teachers. However, I had learned that if anything precluded my having a career in dance, piano would not be my second choice. I would have to find something else.

My piano audition was scheduled for early morning and my dance audition for the afternoon, so Mom put me on a train for New York the preceding night. In my pocket was a check for one night's stay at the YWCA where Mom and I had stayed during spring break. I arrived at the Y with a small white suitcase that held my piano music and my outfits for both auditions. The young woman at the front desk looked horrified when I told her that I had a reservation and asked how old I was. I told her that I was fifteen, and she informed me that the Y didn't take girls under sixteen. "I've stayed here before," I said. "Besides, I have a reservation and a check from my mother." The young woman looked at my written confirmation and Mom's check for five dollars and twenty-cents made out to the YWCA. "Wait here," she said and disappeared. A few minutes later, she informed me that I could stay for one night only and that I couldn't return until I was sixteen. That was fine. All I needed was one night.

I filled out the registration card and reveled in the freedom of traveling alone. I knew that this night was the first of many nights in many hotels that I would experience as a professional dancer, and I could feel the world pulsing with adventure just outside the window. I wanted to run outside and drink in the city's atmosphere, but exploration would have to wait. This trip was about getting into Juilliard, and I wanted a full nine hours' sleep.

The next morning, I woke early, looked through my music, and warmed up my fingers by playing a few excerpts in the air. I walked up to Fifty-Seventh Street and ate a powdered whole-wheat donut and a hot chocolate at Chock Full o' Nuts. I didn't know if there would be food at Juilliard, so I bought a cream cheese sandwich on date-nut bread for lunch.

I knew exactly which subway I had to take because Dad had explained the subway system a few days earlier. While we sat at the dining table after dinner, he drew four sets of parallel tracks. These were the tracks of the two uptown trains and the two downtown trains. Between the two uptown trains was one platform. Between the two downtown trains was the other platform. The local trains ran on the outside tracks, and the express trains ran on the inside tracks. The closest stop to Juilliard was the express stop at 125th Street, but Dad insisted that I take the local train to 116th Street, the stop for Columbia University and Barnard, because he thought that station would be safer, and he gave me walking directions from that stop. I had assumed that when I was standing on the platform among the trains, it would be easy to determine whether I was facing one track or three, but as I walked down the stairs to the platform, two noisy trains zoomed into the station at the same time, one on each side of me. People ran from one to the other, and I couldn't see anything past the two trains. I shouted to a passenger in one of the trains, "Is this the local?" He nodded that it was, and I jumped on board. As the train whizzed uptown, I massaged my fingers to keep them warm, and I squirmed as the metal from my garter belt dug into my thighs. I wished that I could have worn my bobby socks and been comfortable, but Mom said that stockings would make me look older.

Only when the train whizzed past 116th Street did I realize that I was on the express train. At 125th Street, I got off the train, ran up the stairs, crossed over to the downtown side, ran downstairs, and waited and waited and waited. The time for my audition was approaching, so I ran upstairs and hailed a cab. I had only forty-five cents to spare, so I told the driver, "Take me as far as you can for forty-five cents and then point me in the direction of Juilliard." When I got out of the cab, I grabbed my little white suitcase and ran. The cool air made my eyes water, and my left contact lens slid off my pupil and lodged itself under my left eyelid. I arrived at Juilliard at the exact time of my audition, gave the monitor my name, and asked if I could go to the ladies' room to fix my contact lens.

"If you're not here when they call your name, you won't be allowed to audition," she said.

My heart thumped and my mind raced. If only Mom had come with me. She could have explained to the jury that I had a problem with my contact lens and that she was sure that they'd rather wait a few minutes and have me play well, than start on time and have me play badly. But Mom wasn't there, and I didn't doubt that the monitor could deny me an audition. I decided that it was better to play badly—even if it meant that I had to be a dance major—than to risk not playing. Mom would accept a judgment that I didn't have the talent for Juilliard. She wouldn't accept my missing an audition. I tried to push the contact lens back into place and got more and more frustrated as the minutes passed and the lens refused to budge. Finally, my name was called, and I walked onto the stage with my left eyelid flapping like a bat. I was concentrating so hard on keeping the jury from seeing my upstage eye that I failed to check the height of the stool, which was much too low for me. I had 20/15 vision in the right eye with the contact lens and 20/400 vision in the left, so I had no depth perception. As I sat down at the piano, I tried not to move my eyes because I was afraid that the lens might fall out, and the last thing I wanted to do was crawl under the piano to look for the lens that I needed for the dance audition in the afternoon.

I don't remember which parts of which pieces the jury asked me to play—only that the audition was interminable. Every arpeggio seemed to take an hour. Was I playing in slow motion, or had time slowed down the way it does during a car crash? Never in my life had I played so badly in public—not even at my first piano recital when I was six. On that occasion too, time had slowed to a nightmare pace. I knew my short piece backwards and forwards, and I sat down at the grand piano with confidence. But unlike our old York upright piano at home, where I practiced and took my lessons, this piano wasn't missing any ivories. At home, middle C was easy to locate because it was missing the bottom half of the ivory. On this strange piano, all of the keys looked alike. I stared at the keyboard hoping that middle C would somehow reveal itself. Then I heard Mom's voice from her seat in the front row. "Middle C, Lee. Middle C." Now the entire audience thought that I didn't know my starting note! And I still couldn't find it! With as much dignity as I could muster, I stood up, looked at Mom, and said loudly enough for everyone in the auditorium to hear, "I *know* it's middle C. I can't *find* middle C." Mom came up on stage, showed me the note, and I played without making a mistake.

But at Juilliard, Mom wasn't there to bail me out. I was wasting the jury's time, and I blamed myself for not learning how to play without looking at the keys. Finally, after an eternity of banging out Beethoven and Chopin, the jury let me go. I was disappointed that I wouldn't get an accurate assessment of my ability, but I knew that in the long run, the piano audition didn't matter. Even if I went to Juilliard as a dance major, I could probably take classes with a Russian teacher in the evening. And I'd only be in college for a few months.

I located the dance auditorium, ate my cream cheese sandwich, and changed into my leotard. Then I sat by the door. This time I wouldn't be late.

The dance audition was a joy. During the piano audition, besides my contact lens problem, I was competing with unknown pianists. During the dance audition, I could see my competition, and I liked my odds. The piano jury had seemed threatening in the blurry darkness, but the dance jury seemed like a friendly audience, and the choreographer was a supportive bridge between us. I sailed through the ballet combinations, but then the choreographer threw me a curve—modern dance. I had seen bits and pieces of modern dance on television, but I didn't know the technique or the language. The first combination was a jumping step that crossed the stage. I put a big smile on my face that said, "We both know I have no clue what I'm doing," and bounded across the stage leaping as high as I could. The jury laughed, and I knew that it didn't matter what I did for the rest of the afternoon. I had aced the audition in ballet.

As I traveled back to Wilmington on the train, I reflected on the piano audition. I had made so many mistakes, and they had begun long before I sat down at the keyboard. If I had left the hotel earlier, I would have had extra time when I got to Juilliard. If I had asked directions from a subway employee instead of a passenger, I would have taken the right train. If I had stood up to the monitor instead of accepting her word as law, I could have fixed my contact lens. If I had walked onto the stage and explained my problem to the jury, they almost certainly would have given me time to go to the rest room. It was fortunate that I was trained in two disciplines. If piano had been my only talent, my mistakes could have cost me not only Juilliard, but possibly a career. As the train rolled past Philadelphia, I was pretty sure that in three months' time, at the beginning of the school year, I would be a dance major at Juilliard.

But I was wrong.

The results of the Juilliard auditions arrived in the mail. The dance review was a rave: "the jury was unanimous in its opinion that you are an exceptionally talented dancer." The jury praised my technical ability, rhythm, musicality, maturity, and clarity of purpose.

The piano jury, on the other hand, said that my playing was "immature and . . . in need of additional carefully disciplined preparation." The assessment stated that "the tone quality was musical." I had "demonstrated considerable digital facility" and I had "a good feeling for phrase," but only one member of the jury saw me as a professional pianist. I was relieved by the results. The jury's assessment gave Mom no reason to suspect that my audition had been a complete disaster, and she posed no questions about it.

Juilliard scheduled an interview for Mom and me, and we took the train to New York. At the appointed time, Mom and I were ushered into an office where a stone-faced man, "Stonewall," stood behind a massive desk. He indicated that Mom and I should sit in the two chairs facing his desk. Then he turned his attention to Mom. He told her that the dance jury had been very impressed with me and thought I could have a career as a dancer. However, "Juilliard simply can not be responsible for a *child alone* in the city of New York." Mom explained that I was mature for my age and would be an excellent student, but Stonewall emphasized, "We cannot take responsibility for a *child* of *fifteen*. We'd like her to enter our Preparatory Program which is designed for talented *children* like Lee." Every time Stonewall said "child" or "children," I felt two years younger and two inches shorter. Stonewall didn't know that the point of my going to Juilliard was to finish school in one semester, and I knew it wouldn't help to tell him. If I were going to spend two more years in high school, I could stay in Wilmington where I had free housing, an excellent ballet teacher, and a scholarship to an expensive prep school.

Stonewall told Mom that many children in the Preparatory Program did their academic work at the Professional Children's School (PCS), which was located on West Sixtieth Street. PCS had the flexibility to accommodate dance classes, rehearsals, and performances. Before we left, Stonewall looked me in the eye and said, "You're much too *young* to live *alone* in the city of New York."

The minute the door closed behind us, Mom said, "We're going to the Professional Children's School. If we enroll you as a senior, you'll have a high school diploma in May."

The Professional Children's School occupied three floors of a building on Sixtieth Street and overlooked the construction of Lincoln Center and the future site of Juilliard. I liked PCS the minute I walked in the door. It felt like a big house filled with children, rather than a school. As I looked around the lobby, a girl of about twelve ran over to me and asked for my autograph. Seeing my surprise, she asked, "You are Hayley Mills, aren't you?" I was delighted to be mistaken for the teen movie star who had apparently attended PCS while filming a movie. By the time Mom returned with directions to the admissions office, I had learned that two of the von Trapp children in the Broadway show *The Sound of Music* also went to PCS. I liked the idea of going to school with children who were already professionals because it made my own transition from student to professional in the near future seem more feasible.

The woman in the admissions office was much friendlier than the man at Juilliard and talked to both Mom and me. She told us that PCS had ballet students from the School of American Ballet, Ballet Theatre, Ballet Russe, and Ballet Arts. In my classes there would be quite a few ballet dancers including Maria Youskevitch, the daughter of Igor Youskevitch, a *premier danseur* with Ballet Russe and Ballet Theatre. The admissions woman told me that I would have to take Junior English over the summer because New York State required four years of English to graduate. However, I wouldn't have to take French III because my college boards indicated that I could do the work in French IV. PCS had no summer courses, so she recommended Rhodes School, a private school on Fifty-Fourth Street just off Fifth Avenue. The woman gave Mom a brochure for Rhodes School with the words AIR CONDITIONING in huge letters, and on the basis of those two words, I knew I would be happy there during the summer.

In the fall, I would have only four subjects: English, French, Math, and American History, a very light schedule compared to the nine subjects I'd been taking at Tatnall. PCS would schedule my academic classes around my ballet classes once we knew when and where they were.

My escape from the suburbs was taking shape, and just two hours after Stonewall had informed me that I was much too young to live alone in New York, I felt well prepared for the academic year ahead. All I needed now was a great ballet teacher.

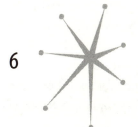

6 At the Ballet Theatre School,
Summer 1961

In 1960, American Ballet Theatre (usually called Ballet Theatre at the time and often called ABT today) became the first American ballet company to tour the Soviet Union. I could imagine the thrill of standing on the Russian stage where *Swan Lake* was born and rehearsing in the studios where Ulanova, Karsavina, and Plisetskaya had trained. Ballet Theatre had stature, exotic tours, and a classical repertoire, three reasons to favor Ballet Theatre and the Ballet Theatre School, but there was also a fourth. The more I thought about SAB and the New York City Ballet, the less I could see myself in an environment apparently dominated by one man.

I had decided to become a professional dancer not only because I loved to dance, but also because dance promised me freedom—physical, emotional, and financial freedom. The older I grew, the more I became aware of the physical restrictions imposed on girls. When Trick and I were small, Dad showed us how to sit cross-legged—"Indian-style," he called it—but a few years later, although I found this a very comfortable position, Dad told me that I could no longer sit cross-legged because the position wasn't proper for a girl. On a sofa, boys could sit comfortably with their legs apart and their arms stretched out along the back of the sofa. They had the right to occupy and demand personal space. They could use their bodies to increase the illusion of power. Girls, on the other hand, had to sit with their knees together, their ankles crossed, and their arms folded in their laps. If they crossed their legs at the knees, they were considered to be deliberately provocative, even a bit trashy. Girls were taught to minimize the amount of space they occupied and to avoid any suggestion of power. In everyday life, I was restricted, but when I put on a leotard and entered a dance studio, I could do anything I pleased. I could spin without having to hold my skirt down. I could turn upside down in a cartwheel without anyone gasping in horror at my lack of decorum, and I could get applause for pulling one foot above my head. Dance allowed me to break free of the physical restraints of the era and to celebrate what my body could do.

Dance also allowed me to break free of the emotional restraints imposed by my family. At home, I was trained to think rather than feel and to present myself as a composed adult. However, when I imagined myself as the White Swan, I could allow myself to be fragile and vulnerable; as Giselle, I could lash out in anger; and as the Black Swan, I could brazenly flirt with a prince. As a dancer, I could break free of the role into which I was born, feel different emotions, and become different people. In one more year, I expected dance to give me financial freedom as well. However, the atmosphere at SAB was not an atmosphere of freedom.

Another attraction of dance was its diversity. When I had taken company class with Ballet Russe, I had loved seeing dancers from many different countries speaking many different languages, but NYCB was becoming less diverse. In the early 1950s, the stars at NYCB came from many different places: Violette Verdy from France, Melissa Hayden from Canada, and Maria Tallchief from California where she had been trained by Bronislava Nijinska. All of these dancers had individual styles which made them unique and fascinating. But for the next generation, my generation, Balanchine was training American dancers with a uniform look and a uniform technique.

With money from the Rockefeller Foundation and the Ford Foundation, Balanchine had scouts looking for talented young girls with the body type he liked (thin girls with long arms and legs and small breasts, preferably tall). The best young dancers were given scholarships to SAB where Balanchine trained them in the style that suited his own choreography. The New York City Ballet dancers of my generation would be less diverse culturally, physically, and stylistically than the generation of the late 1940s and 1950s.

The choreography at NYCB was also becoming less diverse. In the early 1950s, Jerome Robbins had been an important choreographer at the New York City Ballet, but Robbins had left the company, and Balanchine was virtually the only choreographer. Balanchine was prolific, but I wanted the challenge and stimulation of many choreographers and many choreographic styles, so I turned my attention to Ballet Theatre.

The biggest female stars at Ballet Theatre were Lupe Serrano, a Chilean with a flashy technique, and Toni Lander, a Dane with a pure, classic technique. The male stars included the most elegant male dancer of his generation, Erik Bruhn. Adding to its allure, Ballet Theatre had many choreographers and two artistic directors, Lucia Chase and Oliver Smith.

On Mom's instructions, I hadn't told Mr. Jamieson about our plans for New York—although he did know that I had taken a couple of classes at SAB. When Mom told him that I was planning to take a class at Ballet Theatre, he wrote out a letter of introduction to Madame Balieff, the executive director of the school.

The Ballet Theatre School was located on the south side of Fifty-Seventh Street between Eighth and Ninth Avenues, only a few blocks from the Professional Children's School. From the exterior, the building looked like an office building, but when Mom and I got off the elevator, we saw the Ballet Theatre School waiting room on our left. The school didn't have the old world magic of the Metropolitan Opera House, but it felt comfortable—less corporate than SAB. Off the waiting room was a small office where Madame Balieff, round, Russian, and maternal, sat at a cluttered desk. She was engaged in animated conversation in Russian with Madame Pereyaslavec, a short woman who wore her hair on top of her head like a pillbox hat. When Madame Balieff beckoned for me to come into the office, I introduced myself and gave her the note from Mr. Jamieson. "Jimmy!" she said, obviously delighted to see his name. "Jimmy Jamieson! How is he?"

I told her about the Academy of the Dance and *Annie Get Your Gun*, and asked to take an advanced class. Madame Balieff glanced at Madame Pereyaslavec, who gave a barely perceptible nod. "We don't usually allow visitors in Intermediate II," said Madame Balieff, "but since you're a student of Jimmy's, you may take the class today at four-thirty."

"I'd prefer to take an advanced class," I said.

"How old are you?" she asked.

"Fifteen, but I'll be a senior at the Professional Children's School this fall."

"Most of the girls in Intermediate II are sixteen and seventeen. And they've been with Madame Pereyaslavec ever since Intermediate I. But you take Intermediate II, and then we'll see."

Madame Pereyaslavec saw the frustration in my eyes. "Is good class," she said. "Is like Professional. Intermediate II can go directly into company."

I quickly revised my opinion of Intermediate II.

"Go change," said Madame Balieff. "You can't be late."

"Once I close door," said Madame Pereyaslavec, "You stay outside."

I hurried into the dressing room, changed into my leotard, and walked into the main studio. The room was filled with girls in their late teens and one boy. I later learned that the boy was Patrick Adiarte, almost eighteen and already a veteran of two Broadway shows—*The King and I* and *Flower Drum Song*.

The studio entrance door was at the far right end of a wall of mirrors. A grand piano was at the far left end. Opposite the wall of mirrors, above a long, wooden barre, were windows looking north across Fifty-Seventh Street to a neon sign a few blocks away that alternately flashed the time and the temperature. There were also barres on the two shorter walls, but I chose a spot opposite the mirrors so that I could sneak peeks at myself and the other dancers during the barre. (Although teachers regularly admonish dancers not to look at themselves in the mirror, all dancers watch themselves from time to time. The first trick is to glance at the mirror in passing and not distort the line of the movement by staring at the mirror directly. The second trick is to make sure that the teacher doesn't catch you.)

The whispered conversations of the students came to an abrupt halt as Valya Vishnevskaya entered the room, crossed in front of the mirrors, sat at the grand piano, and looked at the doorway. As footsteps approached the doorway, the pianist played a cadenza worthy of Horowitz for the grand entrance of Madame Pereyaslavec, who swept into the room as if it were the stage of the Mariinsky Theatre in St. Petersburg. From the center of the studio, Madame Pereyaslavec surveyed the room. She moved one girl from the center barre to the side barre. Then she moved me two dancers to her left. I had one class to prove that I belonged in Intermediate II, the gateway to the company.

Madame Pereyaslavec demonstrated the pliés, and the barre began. It was a slow barre, so every transition was exposed. In tendus, it was very clear which dancers had the control and the turnout to return the working foot to fifth position in a smooth, seamless motion, and which dancers brought the heel into position first and then used the supporting foot to give them the leverage to turn out the toes. My turnout had vastly improved from my days at Joyce Potter's, but I still didn't have perfect turnout, and in this class it showed.

Madame Pereyaslavec was a ball of energy who wore tap shoes without taps to stomp out the rhythm with her heels. She used French terminology for the steps, counted in Russian, and gave corrections in Russian and English. "Popo eeen!" she said as she tapped my butt, which was sticking out more than some of the other girls. I loved the way she mixed languages and was pleased that she thought me worthy of corrections in my first class.

Ballet students thrive on corrections. It doesn't matter if they are shouted, barked, or non-verbal. Corrections are proof that the student is worth teaching, and being ignored is the student's nightmare. Teachers know this, and sometimes when a student is working well and no correction is necessary, a teacher simply touches the student's fingers as she walks by as a way of saying, "I see you. You're doing well. Don't think I'm ignoring you." Corrections mean that the teacher believes that the student can do better—although as I learned from Mr. Jamieson, not necessarily better in *ballet*.

When I was studying at Joyce Potter's and Anna Marie's, I knew that some mothers gave their daughters ballet lessons so that the girls would become more graceful, develop discipline, and have the cachet of taking ballet, so I divided students into two groups—serious and not serious, with *serious* meaning serious about dance. One day at Mr. Jamieson's, a new boy arrived in class. He appeared to be about college age and had good height in his jumps, but his arms were undisciplined and destroyed his line. After a few weeks, I mentioned to Mr. Jamieson that I thought the boy could be really good if he paid attention to his arms.

"He *is* really good," said Mr. Jamieson. "He's a champion in the high jump. His coach sent him to my class, and our work has already paid off."

This was an eye-opening revelation. Other people could have different, but equally important, goals. Mr. Jamieson showed me that I shouldn't judge other students' progress without knowing their goals.

My goals were clear. In the long term, I wanted to become a dancer who traveled the world. In the short term, I wanted to be accepted into Madame Pereyaslavec's class.

When the barre was over, Madame Pereyaslavec gave a grand gesture toward the window at the piano end of the studio and said, "Lift up!" Then she left the studio, followed by the pianist Valya. Patrick Adiarte, who had taken the barre at the entrance end of the studio, walked the length of the room and raised the window. In Madame Pereyaslavec's class, only the men did the manual labor of lifting the windows and moving the portable barres.

During the break between barre and center, I did several pirouettes to get a feel for the floor. Just as tennis courts and ice rinks can be fast or slow, dance floors can be sticky or slick, rough or uniform. If there is a lot of rosin on the floor, it is sticky and slow. If it has been recently washed, it is slick and fast. I always tested every floor and every stage with multiple pirouettes so that when I had to spin, I knew exactly how much force to take for the required number of turns.

As soon as Madame Pereyaslavec returned to the classroom, Patrick closed the window. I later learned that even on the hottest days, the windows were opened only between barre and center. When a studio is warm, dancers don't need leg warmers or sweatpants, clothing that can disguise and encourage sloppy movement. For example, in the *coup de pied* position, the working foot should wrap around the supporting ankle, but if there is half an inch of fuzzy leg warmer in between the foot and the ankle, the muscle memory will be trained in the looser, less precise position. In Intermediate II, Madame Pereyaslavec didn't allow any leg coverings over tights and allowed tight-fitting sweaters over leotards or tunics only at the barre.

Madame Pereyaslavec placed the girls in group one. Then, group one cleared the floor, and Madame Pereyaslavec set the formation for the rest of the dancers in group two. The lines were staggered so that she could see everyone and everyone could see the mirror. I noticed that while the other girls were waiting to be placed, they stood in a relaxed fifth position, and I followed their lead.

Madame Pereyaslavec treated class like a performance. On stage, when the ballerina is dancing and the dancers in the corps de ballet are watching, the corps dancers can't prop themselves up on the scenery, and in Intermediate II, dancers were not allowed to lean back on the barre. On the one occasion I saw a dancer slump against the barre, Madame Pereyaslavec's eyes flashed in disapproval and her voice sliced through the room like a dagger: "Where you think you are? On *street*?!" The dancer quickly regained her upright position.

In my first class with Madame Pereyaslavec, I was placed in the second row of the second group, but I had no doubt that Madame Pereyaslavec was watching every move I made. I liked being in the second group because that allowed me to watch the best dancers in the class, but I didn't like being in the second row because the girls on either side of me in the front row were a distraction in my peripheral vision, something I wasn't used to because at Mr. Jamieson's, I always stood at the front of the class. On the other hand, the front row girls provided guidelines as to how far each step was supposed to move. For example, when a foot is pointed in front and the dancer is transferring weight onto that foot, some teachers want the toes to stay in place for the transfer. Madame Pereyaslavec required girls to extend the toes forward as they transferred their weight for a bigger, more dramatic move. We all had to move as a corps de ballet and maintain the same distance between girls no matter what the steps might be.

I would soon learn that three of the girls in the front row of the first group were *always* in the front row of the first group: Diana Weber, Sharon Lerit, and Rosie Ricci. Diana Weber, seventeen and a senior in high school, was the perfect package. She was pretty, stood a few inches taller than I, and had a slender, well-proportioned body. She had beautiful line, good turns, and a jump like a gazelle. Sharon Lerit, sixteen and a junior at the Professional Children's School, didn't have as pure a technique as Diana, but she had a compelling personality and an individual style. Sharon was playing the Sad Girl in *Bye, Bye, Birdie* on Broadway. The third girl in the front row was Rosie Ricci, also sixteen and a junior at the Professional Children's School. Rosie was the daughter of concert violinist Ruggiero Ricci. She had strawberry blonde hair, was as short as I and slender as a toothpick. She had a clean technique and did every step without apparent effort. I marveled at her ability to execute triple pirouettes with no apparent preparation.

As I watched these three girls, I believed that I could compete with them technically, but even more encouraging was the fact that the three girls were very different from each other. Diana, with sandy hair, already showed the calm assurance that would one day make her a leading ballerina with the San Francisco Ballet. Sharon, with a long dark braid pulled into a bun for class, seemed to have passion and pain bubbling beneath the surface. And Rosie was a redheaded sprite. There didn't seem to be a mold at Ballet Theatre, and my exuberant personality would add one more color to the palette of the class. As I watched Madame Pereyaslavec, I could see that she would nurture each girl to be the best that she could be without trying to force her into a mold.

Madame Pereyaslavec's combinations in the center were a joy to dance. Her adagio, a slow combination, required flexibility, control, and stamina, and her turns were imaginative. I loved the double inside turns *à la seconde* (one leg extended at 90 degrees, arms in high fifth) which glided into second arabesque in plié (bent supporting knee). Madame Pereyaslavec gave jumps that stayed in place, jumps that traveled across the room, and jumps that moved quickly from side to side. She gave short, almost barked, commands during the jumps. Immediately before a *sisonne,* she might order "three feet," and we were expected to jump exactly thirty-six inches and stick the landing in a perfect arabesque. She prowled the room like a female Napoleon, but under her gruff and demanding exterior, I saw her passion for dance and pride in her students. At the end of the class, Madame Pereyaslavec bowed to the students' applause. With my enthusiastic applause, I told her that I wanted to be a part of the class, and with the approval in her eyes, she told me that I had been accepted.

After I changed back into my street clothes, Mom and I went into Madame Balieff's office where Madame Pereyaslavec and Madame Balieff had already conferred.

"Lee should take the Intermediate II Summer Program," said Madame Balieff, as she handed Mom a brochure. "She will have ballet with Madame Pereyaslavec from one to two-thirty Monday through Friday. At three-thirty, she will have Toe, Character, Variations, or Adagio—nine classes a week. This is limited enrollment for our best students. We usually require girls to wear pink tights and pink shoes, but Lee may wear her black shoes until they wear out. Then you can buy pink. Leotards and tunics may be black, pink, white, or blue."

And that was it. I had just been accepted into the class that led directly into Ballet Theatre, and I had found a teacher who could inspire me to be my best.

With PCS and Ballet Theatre lined up, the next step was to enroll me at Rhodes for Junior English during the summer. The stately Rhodes building, just off Fifth Avenue on Fifty-Fourth Street, was designed by the famous architect Stanford White. It had a uniformed doorman, high ceilings, interior Corinthian columns, and crystal chandeliers. The main lobby had a fireplace, comfortable areas to converse, and a hand-carved oak staircase leading up to the second floor. In the Rhodes brochure, the students looked more sophisticated than the girls and boys at Tatnall and Tower Hill. Instead of knee socks and loafers, the girls at Rhodes wore nylons with either flats or high heels, and some of the students were pictured arm-in-arm as couples. It was clear from the brochure that a superior education was not the only function of this private school. Rhodes also promoted social relationships that would benefit the graduates in their adult lives.

The admissions officer told Mom and me that I would be taking both semesters of Junior English concurrently, and that I would be in school from 9:00 AM to 11:40 AM five days a week from July 5th through August 22nd. Even before Mom and I consulted the train schedule, I knew that I would have to move to New York on July 4th. "Where am I going to live?" I asked.

"I don't know," said Mom, "We'll have to figure that out."

I wondered if I could still perform in Mr. Jamieson's summer musical, *Song of Norway*, which I guessed would have performances on weekends, and Mom said that she'd speak with Mr. Jamieson when we got back to Wilmington.

A few nights later, after the evening class, Mom told me to sit in the waiting room while she talked with Mr. Jamieson in his office. After what seemed like an eternity, Mom stormed out of the office, ordered me to follow her, and barreled out the front door. As I hurried after her, she said, "We're finished with Mr. Jamieson. We're never going to speak to him again. He doesn't care about you or your career. All he cares about is keeping you in Wilmington for the greater glory of *him!*"

I was flabbergasted as I scrambled into the car. I didn't believe for one second that Mr. Jamieson was thinking only of himself, and I knew him better than Mom. If Mr. Jamieson opposed my going to New York, I wanted to know why. But there was nothing I could do. Mom had made her decision, and Mom paid my bills.

During the next year, whenever I came home on weekends, I wished I could take Saturday class with Mr. Jamieson—or at least go to see him, but I didn't dare ask Mom for fear that she would consider my wish to see him a betrayal of her. Mom tended to see people as *for* her or *against* her, and that summer she had decided that Mr. Jamieson was against her.

It was 1969 before I saw Mr. Jamieson again. I was in Wilmington playing the lead role of Laurey in *Oklahoma!* I wasn't very good in the role, and when I saw Mr. Jamieson after one of the performances, I felt awkward and embarrassed. He was with other people, and we exchanged only a few words.

Although I thought of Mr. Jamieson often, I saw him only one more time. In 1991, when I was living in Los Angeles, I received a call from Marsha Zutz Borin, one of my fellow students from Mr. Jamieson's who was organizing a tribute to Mr. Jamieson on the twenty-fifth anniversary of his *Nutcracker* at the DuPont Playhouse. She told me that it would mean a great deal to Mr. Jamieson if I could attend, so I flew to Wilmington for the performance and the gala. Mr. Jamieson danced the role of the grandmother in the first act and was as vibrant and compelling a performer as I had remembered. Joe and Vic both attended the party with their wives. I had seen Joe once on a bus in New York many years earlier, and in the few minutes we had to converse, he told me that he was married to the Academy Award–winning actress Lee Grant. At the gala, I met her for the first time, and she talked about her work as a director. In the following years, Joe, as a producer, and she, as a director, would win many more awards, including an Oscar for Joe. Also in Wilmington for the event was Gemze de Lappe, a warm and wonderful dancer and choreographer who had worked closely with Agnes de Mille and had danced leading roles in de Mille's ballets on Broadway and with Ballet Theatre. Gemze and I had worked together when she re-created the original de Mille choreography for *Oklahoma!* in two productions in which I was a dancer—one at the Paper Mill Playhouse in New Jersey and the other at the New York State Theater in Lincoln Center. At the time of the gala, she was artist-in-residence at Smith College.

Mr. Jamieson was in great demand throughout the party, but when we hugged hello, I felt like the Prodigal Daughter returning home. Two years later, Mr. Jamieson died at the age of seventy-three, nine days after performing the role of the grandmother in *The Nutcracker*.

For the first week of the Ballet Theatre summer program, I commuted daily from Wilmington, but the following week I would be in school, and I needed a place to live. Now that I was a senior, Mom called the YWCA to give it a second try, but when the woman on the telephone asked Mom, "Does your daughter *look* sixteen?" Mom truthfully said that I didn't, and the Y turned me down again. Then we checked out the Barbizon, the most famous residence for women in New York City. Stars like Grace Kelly, Candice Bergen, and Liza Minnelli all lived at the Barbizon at some time, but Mom said it was much too expensive. Finally, Mom found the Hotel Martha Washington, the oldest hotel for women in New York. The Martha Washington, located at 29 East Twenty-Ninth Street, wasn't as convenient to Ballet Theatre as the Y, but it was almost exactly the same price, and I loved it from the first night I stayed there.

Unlike the Y, which was filled with students and tourists, the Martha Washington catered to business and professional women. Every Friday morning when I checked out, the staff wished me a good weekend and asked if I'd be back on Sunday, and every Sunday evening when I checked in, they all welcomed me back. I loved having maid service, and I loved the privacy and freedom of living alone.

Most weekday mornings, I packed my little white suitcase with my textbook and my ballet paraphernalia and took the bus uptown to Rhodes, but some mornings, I got up early so that I could walk up Fifth Avenue and admire the sights. The first landmark I passed was B. Altman & Co., which occupied an entire block on the northeast corner of Fifth Avenue and Thirty-Fourth Street. B. Altman was a department store that catered to the "carriage trade," and the store windows were filled with elegant clothes. I walked around the entire building to make sure I saw every display. The next important store, on the west side of Fifth Avenue at Thirty-Eighth Street, was Lord & Taylor, which was upscale, but trendier than B. Altman. Some of the fashions in Lord & Taylor were considered chic, rather than elegant, and "chic" at this time meant "cool" to the young and "less than elegant" to the old guard. On the fifth floor of Lord & Taylor was a well-appointed ladies' room with a magnificent scale that was absolutely free. I weighed myself at least once a week to make sure I wasn't gaining weight from my Chock Full o' Nuts doughnuts and my potato-and-vegetable dinners at the Automat.

Filling two entire blocks from Fortieth Street to Forty-Second Street was the New York Public Library, which was guarded by two large stone lions: Patience on the south and Fortitude on the north.

At Forty-Ninth Street, I crossed to the east side of Fifth Avenue and circled Saks Fifth Avenue, another high-end clothing store. In the next block, between Fiftieth and Fifty-First Streets, was St. Patrick's Cathedral, the seat of the archbishop of the Roman Catholic Archdiocese of New York. The interior was awe-inspiring and could hold more than two thousand people.

North of St. Patrick's was the white marble home of Best & Co., a store known for women's and children's fashions. This was the store where rich New York mothers shaped the taste of their daughters. Someday, when I was a professional dancer, I hoped that I would shop in all of these stores, but while I was still in school, I was content to admire the architecture and the changing fashions in the windows.

On Fifty-Fourth Street, I walked a few feet west to Rhodes School. The school doorman nodded deferentially when he said, "Good morning" and opened the door for me. I knew that the respect he showed me wasn't because he respected me personally or knew that I was an A student, but because he was paid to act as if Rhodes students were superior. I wondered if he shed his deferential demeanor when he got off work, the way an actor sheds a role when the curtain comes down, or if his daily role became a part of who he was. I could also see how other people might develop a sense of superiority and entitlement because, from the day they are born, people around them are paid to make them feel superior.

Junior English was a literature course, and I was impatient with the classes. In tenth grade, I had studied Shakespeare, Browning, Shelley, and Keats, and I preferred those poets to the ones I was reading that summer: Wordsworth and Longfellow. When I read Wordsworth's "Intimations of Immortality" in which he wrote that babies come "trailing clouds of glory," I decided that Wordsworth had never seen a baby up close. In my experience, if babies were trailing anything, it was spit-up or poop. My lack of interest in Junior English undoubtedly had something to do with the fact that right outside my classroom the city of New York was pulsing with life. Star dancers were preparing for the Professional class with Madame Pereyaslavec, and I was trapped behind a desk.

As soon as my class at Rhodes was dismissed, I walked back to Fifth Avenue and continued north to Fifty-Seventh Street, the corner of conspicuous consumption. On the southeast corner was Tiffany & Co., the epitome of excellence in diamonds and sterling silver. Even the turquoise Tiffany boxes were status symbols. Just south of Tiffany was Bonwit Teller, a department store that had tiny purple flowers on its shopping bags. And just west of Fifth Avenue on Fifty-Seventh Street was Henri Bendel, the store that introduced Coco Chanel's designs to America. Henri Bendel's elegant brown-and-white striped shopping bags were proof that the bearer had only one degree of separation from Paris, the fashion capital of the world.

As I walked west along Fifty-Seventh Street, I walked from the domain of the rich to the domain of the artists. As much as I liked the glamorous shops, I liked the theatres more, and in the theatre district, I already felt at home.

Between Sixth and Seventh Avenues, I passed Steinway Hall, which was both a concert hall and a retail store for the best-known pianos in America. Steinway Hall represented the road not taken. At Seventh Avenue was Carnegie Hall, which I knew from the old joke, "How do you get to Carnegie Hall? Practice." Upstairs in the Carnegie Hall building were the dance studios of Ballet Arts, where many Russian teachers, including Sonia Wojcikowska, Madame Antonova's daughter, gave ballet classes. When I arrived at Eighth Avenue and Fifty-Seventh Street, I walked a short block north to the Automat to buy lunch and begin my homework.

Inside the Automat, I went directly to the centrally located kiosk to change quarters or a dollar bill into nickels because the food behind the glass windows and the hot chocolate and coffee machines required nickels. I loved choosing my food, choosing my table, and being allowed to sit and study for as long as I wanted. The clientele ranged from business people to the homeless. I enjoyed looking around the room and trying to figure out what people did for a living. Did they sell insurance? Work in an advertising agency? Deliver newspapers? Was the couple in the corner a pair of lovers whispering sweet nothings, or were they partners in crime confirming the details of their next heist? The possibilities were endless. Sometimes, people in dirty, tattered clothes stirred ketchup into a glass of water to make tomato juice, or squeezed fresh lemon slices into a glass with sugar and water to make lemonade. The Automat employees allowed them to stay as long as they didn't disturb the other diners. On the East Side, I saw people born into mind-boggling luxury. At the Automat, I saw people who slept on sidewalks.

Madame Pereyaslavec's ballet classes were relentless, and I learned to pace myself by peeking at the neon clock outside the studio. If she began the big jumps fifteen minutes before the end of class, I could dance every step full-out, but if she began the big jumps ten minutes earlier, I had to conserve energy because appearing out of breath or showing visible fatigue was unacceptable. Madame Pereyaslavec (Madame Perey) wanted her students to be "strong like bull," and her classes were the most physically demanding I ever took.

After Madame Perey's ballet class, we had a one-hour break before the second class, which varied day to day. Toe, Variations, and Adagio were all on pointe, but the Character class required shoes with heels. Character class was fun, but most of us didn't want to be labeled "character dancers" because character dancers have less prestige than ballerinas and don't dance the meaty classical roles.

In Toe class, we worked on technique, and in Variations, we learned classical variations from traditional ballets. The steps that looked the simplest were sometimes the most difficult because they required superior control, and every movement was exposed. In the flashier variations, there was a greater margin for error. (For example, if a dancer is simply balancing in passé, any imperfection, such as a sickled foot, is more obvious than if the dancer is leaping or spinning in the same position.) I liked the flashy variations because I was self-conscious about my body and wanted people to concentrate on what it was doing, not how it looked. I had muscular thighs, and my breasts were straining against a B-cup bra. (An A-cup was considered perfect.) I had a big bottom lip, which I thought was too big for my face, and my feet were short and wide like a duck and had a gentle arch. My feet were well-designed for balance and strength, but not considered as visually pleasing as slender feet with a high arch. I was more secure in my technique than in my appearance.

I was not the only girl self-conscious about her body. Some girls put Saran

Wrap under their tights to try to reduce their thighs. One girl, determined to get rid of every ounce of fat, became so thin that Madame Pereyaslavec told her that she had three weeks to put on five pounds or she would be barred from the class until she had gained weight. Another realized that she had an odor problem when Madame Pereyaslavec announced, "Is girl in class must buy deodorant." We were all trying to shape our instruments and find our optimal weight at a time when our bodies were still growing and changing.

The most difficult class was Adagio, the class in which we worked with boys. The only partner I'd ever had was Mr. Jamieson, and with him, the process was simple. He told me what to do; I did it, and then we refined the movement. In Adagio class at the Ballet Theatre School, the boys were less experienced, didn't know where to place their hands, and sometimes pushed the girls off balance. Diana, with her perfect body, was the best in the class at adagio, and Rosie, who weighed less than a feather, seemed easy to lift. Sharon and I had more difficulty because we were not only a few pounds heavier, but we both carried weight in our thighs, which gave us a lower center of gravity, and the lower the center of gravity, the harder the person is to lift. Also, when the boys were taught where to place their hands, they were taught the positions for perfectly proportioned girls. In time, I learned to tell my partners that they needed to position their hands a bit lower on me than on most girls.

During the first few weeks of the summer program, I had blisters on my toes because I had lost the habit of wearing toe shoes. At Joyce Potter's and Anna Marie's, I had worn toe shoes for every ballet class, and I had been as comfortable in toe shoes as I was in bedroom slippers. Madame Swoboda and the Philadelphia Dance Academy both required ballet slippers, but while I was studying with them, I still had several classes a week on pointe with Anna Marie. However, when I moved to Mr. Jamieson's, I wore ballet slippers for most of the class and did pointe work for only a few minutes at the end, so my toes had grown soft. I was no longer as comfortable or as secure in toe shoes as I had been when I was younger.

That summer, I also learned that Capezio made a seemingly endless variety of toe shoes. The shank could be strong or medium or light. The box could be tapered or nearly straight. The vamp could be long or short. I loved going into the Capezio store, which had stacks and stacks of pink boxes with a great range of styles and sizes. The most glamorous boxes were the ones with the names of ballerinas written on the end in black marker. Inside these boxes were the custom-made shoes of the stars. At Mr. Jamieson's, I had begun wearing Nicolini, a shoe which was a bit more pliable than Duro-Toe, and I stayed with Nicolini throughout my senior year.

During the delightfully long days of summer, I spent my mornings in school. In the afternoons, I had two wonderful dance classes and time to chat with the other students. In the evenings, I had dinner at the Automat and rode the bus or walked back to the Martha Washington hotel. At night, as the sky grew dark, I finished my homework and read books from the Wilmington Public Library. My life was just about perfect. But that was about to change.

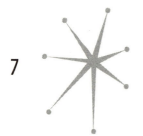

7   # Stars in Madame Pereyaslavec's Class, 1961–1962

Mom told me that it would be "nicer" for me to live with a family in New York. In fact, Dad had already enlisted the help of our minister at St. Andrew's to find a family in Manhattan who had a piano and room for a budding ballerina. Shortly thereafter, Mom informed me that a New York minister and his wife, who had just had their first baby, were interested in meeting me at their home in a nice residential district. The family lived in a three-bedroom apartment above the church, and the church had a grand piano I could play every morning before school.

My transition from the Martha Washington hotel to the apartment of the Reverend and Mrs. consisted of a mating dance in three steps. First, I visited the couple and proved that I knew how to hold a baby and change diapers. Second, the Reverend wrote to Mom and Dad and told them that the "going rate" for me to stay with them in the fall would be eighty-five dollars a month (fifteen dollars a month less than the Martha Washington). The Reverend also wrote that the relationship between them and me should be similar to that of an uncle and aunt to a niece. Finally, on their way back to New York after their summer vacation, the Reverend and Mrs. stopped at our home in Wilmington where they met Mom, Dad, Trick, Twink, and Tuck. The details of my living with them were finalized. Mom and Dad would pay them eighty-five dollars a month. I would babysit whenever they went out in the evening, and they would provide me with a sweet roll in the morning and dinner at night.

The September days were getting shorter, and it was already dark when I arrived at the church for my first week with the minister and his wife. The neighborhood was lovely, but I missed the lighted lobby and friendly staff of the Martha Washington as I found my way upstairs to the minister's apartment. Mrs. was a serious young woman who seemed consumed by her responsibilities. I could feel her tension as she led me down the hall to the room where I would stay during the week, a room her husband had been using as a study. Across the hall was the bathroom I would share with the Reverend.

I was still unpacking when Mrs. called me in to dinner. The dining room was deserted, so I looked into the kitchen where three places were set at a small kitchen table. I was surprised to see that we were eating in the kitchen because the adjacent dining room looked quite comfortable. At home, Mom used the kitchen table for feeding babies, who ate before the rest of the family, and for helping children with schoolwork while she was cooking or baking. Once we were old enough to feed ourselves, we ate all of our meals, including breakfast, in the dining room. I hoped that Mrs. had just oiled the dining table and that we would eat in the dining room in the future. The kitchen was a big step down from the Automat.

Mrs. spooned some canned fruit cocktail around a scoop of cottage cheese, and put the plate in front of the Reverend. Then she asked me, "How much fruit do you want?"

At home, fruit cocktail was dessert, but the luncheon specials at Woolworth's five-and-dime featured fruit cocktail as a first course, so I said, "Just a spoonful." I didn't want to fill up before the main course.

As we ate our cottage cheese and fruit cocktail, Mrs. talked about the beautiful baby clothes that friends, family, and parishioners had given their baby when she was born. The Reverend thought they should give away many of them since the baby couldn't possibly wear them all before she outgrew them, but I could see that Mrs. didn't agree and that the Reverend already knew his wife's position. The couple did agree that the monthly check from my parents would be a big help now that they had a baby. They asked about my classes at Ballet Theatre, and I told them about Madame Pereyaslavec, Intermediate II, and the stars who took the morning class. Since the Reverend had the most food, I paced myself to finish my fruit cocktail at the same time he did.

"Your mother told me that you like ice cream for dessert," said Mrs. "Would you like some now, or would you like to get it later?"

Whoops. Cottage cheese and fruit cocktail were the main course. I opted for ice cream immediately. The Reverend left the kitchen, and Mrs. did the dishes while I ate my ice cream.

The following evening when I arrived at the apartment, Mrs. informed me that I would eat in my room from now on because "dinner is the only time I have alone with my husband—the only time we can really talk. Besides," she said, "your fork clinks against your plate when you eat, and it's very irritating."

I felt as if I had been slapped. All my life, people had complimented me on my table manners, and the preceding night, I had been particularly careful. But from that night on, I ate dinner alone in my room.

In the mornings, I didn't see the couple when I got my sweet roll from the kitchen. In the evenings, I saw Mrs. when she called me into the kitchen to get a tray with a TV dinner or a pot pie. On the few occasions when Mrs. gave dinner parties during the week, she offered me the same food she would later serve to her guests, but I was never invited to eat in the dining room.

I soon learned that my clinking fork wasn't my only defect. I didn't scrub out the bathtub properly. I didn't answer the phone properly. I didn't become friends with the nanny of her friend who lived nearby, and when Mrs. asked me to leave ballet class early because she and her husband had an important dinner party, I refused. She insisted. I suggested that she ask her friend's nanny to bring her baby over to the apartment for an hour until I got home. I also offered to take a cab instead of a bus if she would pay for it, but I would *not* leave class early. I was in New York to become a dancer, not a nanny.

I remember only one real conversation with the Reverend. I had been home sick all day, and Mrs. was taking a nap when the Reverend came home. He stopped in to see how I was feeling, and we talked for a few minutes about tropical fish. He said that he liked watching them because he found them relaxing. I told him that my brothers had tropical fish, and that I had found them relaxing until one day, shortly after she gave birth, Mama Mollie devoured her babies. The voice of Mrs. interrupted our conversation. "Where are you?" she called down the hall.

"I'm talking with Lee," he called back.

"Don't waste your time," she said. "I need you in here."

And that was the end of our conversation.

I could see that escaping the suburbs required more than merely living in New York City. I suspected that the life of Mrs. was similar to that of my mother when I was a baby—diapers, spit-up, and worries about money. Like Mom, Mrs. depended upon her husband for financial support and social status. Like Mom, she seemed nervous and overworked. Like Mom, if her husband were transferred to another city, she would have to leave her home and move with him. The preceding summer, I had tasted the life of a dancer: ballet class to begin the day, variations and adagio and character dance in the afternoon, dinners at the Automat, and nights at the theatre or in a nice hotel with maid service and the freedom to come and go as I wished. My step back into a traditional, male-centric environment simply confirmed my determination to live in the freer, more inclusive community of dance.

At the Ballet Theatre School, I felt at home. Madame Pereyaslavec was inspiring and encouraging; Madame Balieff was warm and motherly, and Rosie became my best friend. Some mornings, Rosie and I would meet at the corner drugstore before school for sweet cherry Cokes, with lots of cherry syrup. Sometimes we had lunch together at the Automat or the Crest Cafeteria before the Intermediate II class at four-thirty. Several times, I went to Rosie's house in New Jersey, and she came to mine in Wilmington.

A few years later, when I was dancing with the Metropolitan Opera Ballet, Rosie was dancing with Ballet Theatre. And in 1971, after I had left ballet for Broadway, we sang and danced together in the Alan Jay Lerner musical *Lolita, My Love*, which was Broadway-bound, but closed in Boston.

In *Lolita, My Love*, Rosie and I played schoolmates of fourteen-year-old Lolita. During the Boston run, Rosie and I went to a cast party at the elegant Ritz-Carlton Hotel. Outside the entrance to the hotel restaurant was a large sign stating that pants were not acceptable on women and mini-skirts were acceptable only on teenagers. As we approached the entrance in our mini-skirts, Rosie whispered just loudly enough for the maitre d' to hear, "It's a good thing we're teenagers." Even up close, we could pass for schoolgirls.

I looked particularly youthful that evening because I was wearing an orange skirt and vest ensemble that was a children's size ten that I had acquired from performing in the Milliken Breakfast Show, part of an annual convention for Milliken & Company, which had early morning performances in the ballroom of the elegant Waldorf Astoria hotel on Park Avenue. The Milliken Show paid Broadway salaries, and the schedule was designed to accommodate dancers who were performing eight shows a week on Broadway. The producers even provided limousines to drive the performers from rehearsals to their theatres for matinees. In 1970, Stanley Prager, director of *Come Blow Your Horn*, *Minnie's Boys*, and *Don't Drink the Water*, was the director, and Danny Daniels, choreographer of *All-American*, *High Spirits*, and later *The Tap Dance Kid*, was the choreographer. During morning rehearsals, the producers provided orange juice, coffee, and Danish pastries. After lunch, they provided huge boxes of chocolates. On performance days, the Waldorf Astoria laid out a continental breakfast buffet with waiters to serve us, and after the show closed, the performers were allowed to keep their clothes—the latest fashions in the latest Milliken fabrics. The Milliken Breakfast Show was both lucrative and a boost for the ego because dancers were not usually given so many perks. The competition was even fiercer than for a Broadway show because the talent pool included dancers committed to their current shows as well as dancers who were looking for jobs.

I was too small to wear adult sizes, so I auditioned as a Millikiddie.

There were three sizes of Millikiddies—children's sizes six, eight, and ten, and at ninety-two pounds, I was a perfect size ten. Baayork Lee had set the precedent of an adult playing a child, and I followed in her footsteps and performed as a Millikiddie, size ten, along with two eleven-year-olds and a fourteen-year-old. Five years later, Baayork Lee created the role of Connie in *A Chorus Line* and told her own story, the story of a dancer who wanted to become a ballerina but was too short for ballet companies and at the age of thirty-two was still being cast as a child. During the Los Angeles run of the original national company (which included most of the original Broadway cast), Baayork took a leave of absence to mount the Australian company, and I became the Connie telling much the same story—although when I performed the role, I wasn't Connie Wong who had performed in *The King and I*, but Connie McKenzie who had performed in summer stock. *A Chorus Line* was the first time Baayork and I worked together, but we already knew each other from auditions.

At the Ballet Theatre School, Rosie was my most direct competition because we were the same height, about the same age, and focused on ballet rather than Broadway, but in dance, it is quite common for competitors to become best friends because they take class together, audition together, and are often hired by the same dance companies and the same shows. Dancers who are similar in size and type get to know each other's abilities and recommend each other when offered jobs they can't do themselves. In film and television, from *All About Eve* to *Smash*, actors and understudies sabotage each other to get roles, but in my experience, dancers are usually very supportive of each other. They lend each other music and costumes, teach each other choreography, and share insights about choreographers and directors and companies. Many dancers remain friends long after their dance careers have ended.

It has been many years since I danced professionally, but most of my friends are or were dancers, singers, or triple threats (singer/dancer/actors). My past, current, and future support system comes from individual performers and from dance organizations: Career Transition for Dancers, St. Mary's College of California's LEAP program (a BA program in major cities which is designed specifically for working and retired dancers), and the performers' unions: Actors' Equity Association for theatre, SAGAF-TRA for film and television, and the American Guild of Musical Artists for opera and ballet companies. There is a fourth performers' union, the American Guild of Variety Artists, which covers nightclubs, cabaret, and comedians, but I never worked under AGVA's jurisdiction because all of the shows in which I performed in the United States, including shows in Las Vegas, were book shows—plays or musicals, rather than cabaret, so I was covered by Actors' Equity. As of 2013, all four unions have pension and health benefits.

One of many reasons that dancers bond together is that dancers are no-mads. They learn to make friends quickly, leave them for years, and pick up again where they left off. Through mutual friends, reviews, programs, and now social media, dancers know what their colleagues are doing even when they are halfway around the world. When I began rehearsals for the Broadway musical *Meet Me in St. Louis* in 1989, I had been living in Los Angeles for thirteen years, but when I walked into the New York offices of Actors' Equity, Sam's restaurant, and the stage doors of Broadway theatres, people welcomed me back as if I'd been away for only a short time, and on the opening night of *Meet Me in St. Louis*, I was awarded the Gypsy Robe—an honor which is given to the singer or dancer who has the most Broadway shows and personifies the dedication and professionalism of the Broadway gypsy. I had been gone, but was not forgotten.

My nomadic career included ballet companies, opera companies, musical theatre, films, episodic television, industrials (shows for conventions), and television commercials. I danced in Europe, Africa, and America. Some dancers stay in one discipline, such as ballet, but move from company to company, but even dancers who spend most of their careers with one company usually leave their homes for extensive tours and moonlight with other companies or in other media.

The same week that I met the Reverend and his wife, I saw my first show on Broadway, *Bye, Bye, Birdie*, an exuberant musical comedy about a teenage girl who wins a kiss from a sexy rock and roll singer, Conrad Birdie, who is about to join the Army. (Conrad Birdie looked remarkably like Elvis Presley whose induction into the Army in 1958 was a media event called "black Monday" by his fans.) Sharon Lerit, from Madame Perey's Intermediate II class, was playing the role of the Sad Girl, the girl whose dismay at Conrad Birdie's induction provoked the leading man to sing "Put on a Happy Face." On stage, Sharon was as natural and compelling a performer as she was in the studio. *Bye, Bye, Birdie* had a large chorus of teenage singers and dancers, and I thought it would be fun to dance in a Broadway musical, but there were three reasons why I decided to keep my focus on ballet. Two were valid. One was not.

First, classical ballet dancers got more respect than Broadway dancers, who were sometimes called chorines, gypsies, or (if they tap danced) hoofers. Since my gender defined me as a second-class citizen in many people's eyes, respect was important to me. Second, in a ballet company, a great dancer could dance leading roles and become a star, but on Broadway, a great dancer stayed in the chorus unless she was also a good singer and a good actress, and I didn't know if I could sing or act. Third, Broadway shows could open and close in a week, so there was no steady paycheck. In ballet, I believed (incorrectly) that there was.

Today, musicals run for decades, but in 1961, only two musicals, *My Fair Lady* (1956–1962) and *Oklahoma!* (1943–1948), had broken the five-year mark. *Bye, Bye, Birdie* was considered a hit with a run of a year and a half. However, that same season, *Kean* and *All-American* ran for less than three months even though the leading men in both shows (Alfred Drake and Ray Bolger) received Tony nominations. (The Tony Awards are the Oscars of Broadway.) Every time a Broadway show closed, all of the dancers had to audition for new jobs, so there was no job stability. In ballet, I saw the same dancers in the same companies year after year, so I assumed that ballet dancers were employed full-time. I knew that the stars sometimes danced with several companies in the course of a year, but I assumed that they did this to broaden their artistic experience. It didn't occur to me that ballet dancers scrambled to find interim jobs during layoffs just to pay the rent.

When the Ballet Theatre summer program ended, I joined my family for our annual vacation at the beach in Wildwood Crest, New Jersey. I enjoyed walking the beach, riding the waves, and playing Skee Ball on the Boardwalk, but I was eager to get back to New York—back to the center of the universe of American dance.

My immediate goal was to get into Madame Pereyaslavec's morning class. None of the other girls from Intermediate II took this class, and to the best of my knowledge, none of the dancers in the Professional class were still in school, but I thought that taking class with professionals would be inspiring and would give me additional insight into the ballet world. I decided that my best chance of getting into the class was to show up at the Ballet Theatre School at eleven-fifteen and ask Madame Balieff if I could take the class at eleven-thirty.

My first morning back in New York, I walked into the waiting room and saw three other dancers lined up outside Madame Balieff's office. Five minutes later, the line hadn't moved. This was a problem because the only dancers who entered class without paying were company members, so I needed to pay before class. Also, Madame Perey's Professional class, like Intermediate II, almost always began on time, and once the door was closed, no one entered. I was wondering if I should change into my leotard when Madame Balieff called out, "Lee, I know you. Hurry and change!" That quickly, I was in the Professional class.

The class that morning and every succeeding morning lived up to my high expectations. Madame Pereyaslavec dominated the room as she did in Intermediate II. She placed people at the barre and in the center, and she called out the steps. For quick steps, her commands were clipped, but for legato movements, she extended her words: "arrrrrrabesssssque, proomenaaaaade." However, unlike Intermediate II, which had the same students day after day, the Professional class had a dazzling, ever-changing array of talent.

When Ballet Theatre was in New York, Eleanor D'Antuono, Gayle Young, and Richard Wagner were some of the company members who took the eleven-thirty class. Richard Wagner once made the mistake of walking into the room wearing a grey sweatshirt with a black drawing of Beethoven on the front. Madame Perey did not allow red, green, or prints in her classes, and even the subtle black drawing was too much. After her grand entrance, she surveyed the room and addressed Richard Wagner: "You have plain shirt?" she asked. Wagner said that he did. "No red. No green. We wait," said Madame Perey. She moved a couple of people at the barre; Richard Wagner returned in a white t-shirt, and class began.

Quite a few of the principal dancers from the New York City Ballet appeared in Madame Pereyaslavec's morning class, but it was rare to see a dancer from the NYCB corps de ballet. The generally accepted rumor was that Balanchine did not like his dancers to study at other schools, and only the stars were secure enough to defy him. In Madame Perey's class, the NYCB dancers included Violette Verdy, Maria Tallchief, Patricia Wilde, Sara Leland, Mimi Paul, and Jillana. Jillana was the prototypical Balanchine ballerina—tall, with long arms and legs, beautiful line, and clean technique. She came to class with a tiny dog in her dance bag—Tiger. Like most dogs belonging to dancers, Tiger stayed perfectly still during the class, but sat up when he heard the ending applause. Only after Jillana called his name did he hop out of the bag and scurry after her as she left the studio.

The most exciting classes were those with the superstars: Margot Fonteyn, Maria Tallchief, and Rudolf Nureyev. My idol was Fonteyn. She was unassuming in class, but even the other ballerinas treated her with deference. The first time I saw Margot Fonteyn in class, Madame Perey placed her first and indicated the center spot of the first group. "You stand here?" said Madame Perey with an atypical question mark at the end of her sentence. Fonteyn glanced toward the spot nearest the piano. "Or maybe here," said Madame Perey decisively as she indicated the spot on the far left. From that day forward, whenever Fonteyn was in class, Madame Perey always placed her on the far left next to the piano. Unlike dancers who compete with each other and spur each other on, Fonteyn seemed to work in her own universe. Instead of reaching out to the audience, she pulled the audience in to her. Fonteyn's extensions (the height she lifted her legs) weren't as high as the other dancers, and she appeared to be working not to increase the range of her technique, but to maintain and perfect it. In 1961, Margot Fonteyn was in her early forties, and this method of working was typical for dancers her age, but I didn't know that at the time. To me, Margot Fonteyn was ageless.

Maria Tallchief, on the other hand, was a strong, outgoing dancer with regal bearing—consistent with her position as America's most famous ballerina and the daughter of an affluent chief of the Osage Nation. Tallchief gave the impression that she could dance anything. Watching Fonteyn and Tallchief side by side was a study in contrast, but both had one thing in common: they were unique. Neither dancer could be confused with anyone else. (A year or so later, when I met Marjorie Tallchief in France, I realized what a smart move it had been for the sisters to work on different continents because the women were only two years apart in age and had a strong family resemblance.)

During this year, and for the rest of the decade, the biggest *male* star in ballet was Rudolf Nureyev, who made headlines when he defected from the Soviet Union in Le Bourget Airport in Paris on June 16, 1961. In the following months, while I was in the Ballet Theatre summer program, he was dancing in Europe, but in January of 1962, halfway through my senior year at the Professional Children's School, Nureyev danced with Maria Tallchief on the *Bell Telephone Hour* television show. This was his first performance in the United States. Nureyev was only twenty-three years old and had not yet been featured on the cover of *Time* magazine, but his fame already transcended the dance world. When he walked into Madame Pereyaslavec's class, I wasn't the only dancer trying not to gape. His presence dominated the room the way Michelangelo's *David* dominates the Accademia Gallery in Florence. Nureyev projected an animalistic arrogance with a keen intelligence. His jumps and turns were breathtaking, but his technique was sometimes sloppy: instead of spinning high on demi-pointe, he sometimes pumped up and down so that his heel came close to the floor in mid-pirouette, and his pirouette preparations were often halfway between second and fourth positions. When Madame Pereyaslavec gave him corrections, he maintained his arrogant bearing, but his appreciation and hunger to learn were apparent in his eyes. His body seemed designed to dance, and yet his legs were shorter than the ideal. He was a mass of compelling contradictions, and like other superstars, he was unique. When he and Margot

Fonteyn became partners, it was a marriage made in heaven. She gave the partnership elegance and vulnerability. He gave it youth and bravura.

My observation that stars had a unique appearance as well as style was both encouraging and discouraging. While I was growing up, Mom repeatedly told me that I would have to be good enough to be a ballerina because I was too short for the corps, and I knew that I didn't look like the typical corps dancer. I was shorter, curvier, and more exuberant. This made me unique, which was good because I wanted to dance leading roles. On the other hand, the way into a ballet company seemed to be through the corps, and that required not sticking out. My uniqueness was not so good. This paradox was problematic, and my concern about how I should look was exacerbated by an excellent dancer who was a regular in the Professional class.

The young woman was taller than I, older than I, and carried a few more pounds than most ballet dancers. She had a strong technique and an individual style. Madame Pereyaslavec obviously liked her because she placed her in the first row of the first group unless there was an entire row of company dancers. I overheard that the girl had auditioned for Ballet Theatre, but hadn't gotten into the company because Lucia Chase didn't like her. Since I thought the girl was terrific, her apparent lack of success frightened me.

I had known since childhood that it is possible to be too short or too tall for a ballet company. However, when I was a senior in high school, I didn't realize that it is possible to be a perfectly acceptable height, but just not the height that the company needs to replace. Companies often try to hire dancers the same size as a departing dancer because it saves money on rehearsal time. The new dancer can fill the same positions as the departing dancer without moving the other dancers around. Also, certain costumes are made for tall dancers and won't be cut down, and others are made for short dancers and don't have enough material for taller dancers. There are many reasons why a first-rate dancer might not be offered a contract at an audition, but I didn't know that until I began working professionally.

With graduation only a few months away, I wondered how much the members of Ballet Theatre were paid, but my parents, like many parents in the 1950s, had taught me never to discuss money, sex, religion, or politics outside of the family, so I thought it would be rude to ask anyone about salaries. Also, I didn't want to appear mercenary. Then I noticed that one of the male dancers in Ballet Theatre regularly came to class with a hand towel from the Hotel Rodney, a very nice hotel with a gym and a pool that was just across Fifty-Seventh Street from Ballet Theatre. Since the dancer was in the corps de ballet, I naively concluded that a corps salary would cover the cost of an expensive hotel.

In early spring, eight months after my first class with Madame Pereyaslavec, Lucia Chase watched part of the Intermediate II class. Even if I hadn't recognized her from photographs, I would have known that she was important because she entered the studio *during* the class. She was obviously there to see Diana, and from the whispered conversation between Ms. Chase and Madame Pereyaslavec, I concluded that Diana would probably get into the company that spring. I also concluded that Ms. Chase was not interested in anyone else at that time. Sharon and Rosie still had another year of high school, so I thought that I was probably next in line from the Intermediate II class, but there was no guarantee that the next dancer would come from that class or that Ballet Theatre would need another dancer in the near future.

During this year in New York, my ties to people and things outside of dance faded away. I was certainly not a part of the minister's family, but I was losing touch with my own. I felt like a visitor when I went to Delaware on the weekends, and I quit piano lessons because piano seemed pointless and time-consuming. I wrote to Mom and told her that if I didn't get into a ballet company by fall, I wanted to study academic subjects at Barnard and take class with Madame Perey until I could join Ballet Theatre or Ballet Russe.

However, that spring Mom made an announcement that forced me to reconsider my options: my family was moving to Geneva, Switzerland, where Dad would be Product Supervisor for DuPont International. Dad would begin his three-year stint (which actually lasted four years) in May, but he would fly home in late June, and the family would sail first class on the S. S. *United States* on June 29th. If I wanted to stay in New York, the DuPont company would pay my way to Switzerland once a year. In addition, the family would come back to the States for a couple of weeks every summer. Mom told me that I could stay in New York or go to Switzerland. It was entirely up to me, but she needed to know my decision soon.

I was enchanted by the idea of sailing on one of the largest, most glamorous ships at sea. I could envision the elegant surroundings, the gourmet food, and the formal attire at dinner. I wanted to see the Eiffel Tower, the Arc de Triomphe, and the Swiss Alps. One reason I had decided to become a dancer was to see the world, and this was my chance to see Europe, but my decision had to be based on what was best for my career.

During the 1950s and 1960s, corporate money was changing the dance landscape in America. The seeds were sown in the 1930s, when Lincoln Kirstein, the well-connected heir to Filene's department store money, decided to found an American ballet company and brought George Balanchine to the United States. Kirstein and Balanchine co-founded the School of American Ballet and the short-lived American Ballet. Kirstein continued to pursue his dream of an American company with another short-lived company, Ballet Caravan, while Balanchine choreographed for Ballet Russe, Hollywood films, Broadway musicals, and even a ballet for elephants for the Ringling Bros. Circus. In 1946, after Kirstein got out of the army, he personally provided much of the financing for his and Balanchine's new company, Ballet Society. At this time, the United States was celebrating the success of "our boys" in World War II, and veterans were going to college and buying homes, farms, and businesses on the GI Bill. As women were pushed into the home, the status of women dropped. (A 2012 study of pronoun use in 1.2 million U.S. books, 1900–2008, indicated that the status of women is reflected in the ratio of male to female pronouns in written language. From 1900 to 1945, the ratio was 3.5 to 1. From 1946 to 1967, it was 4.5 to 1, a two-decade drop beginning the year I was born.) Concurrent with the increased status of men compared to women, the patriotism of the war years continued into the 1950s during the Cold War with Russia.

In the late 1940s, Kirstein and Balanchine did two things that helped them ride the wave of patriotism and increased the viability of their new company. First, in 1946, Balanchine got divorced from foreign-born Vera

Zorina and married the American ballerina Maria Tallchief, who was dancing with Ballet Russe. This new marriage brought Balanchine publicity at
the time he was establishing his new company and guaranteed that Tallchief
would soon be dancing the premieres of his ballets and would be on his arm
at social events. In her autobiography and in the video *Dancing for Mr. B: Six
Balanchine Ballerinas*, Tallchief said that she was "a very immature young
girl" when Balanchine surprised her with his marriage proposal, but Balanchine assured her that it didn't matter if she didn't love him or if the marriage didn't last. Tallchief said she was "unsophisticated about many things,"
but she understood that she was a "fundamental part" of Balanchine's plan
for his new company and that the marriage was "a working arrangement."
(Six years later, the marriage was annulled.)

The second important event was that Kirstein and Balanchine changed
the name of their company from Ballet Society to the New York City Ballet.
This positioned NYCB as the home team in an affluent city and highlighted
the fact that Ballet Russe sounded Russian (politically incorrect during the
Cold War) and that Ballet Theatre showcased mostly foreign stars. Kirstein's
dream of an American ballet company had found its time in the patriotism
of the 1950s.

Kirstein secured money from the Rockefeller Foundation and the Ford
Foundation for SAB and NYCB. This money financed scouting expedi-
tions to cities all around the country and gave SAB scholarships to the most
promising young dancers. These grants also allowed Balanchine to hire stars
away from Ballet Theatre and Ballet Russe, which was demoralizing and
destabilizing for those two companies. Eventually, as Lynn Garafola wrote
in *Legacies of Twentieth-Century Dance*, "Ford largesse made it possible for
Kirstein and the New York City Ballet to claim—and ultimately control—
the New York State Theatre [*sic*]."

In the spring of 1962, when I had to choose between staying in New York
and going to Europe, the New York State Theater (the new, state-of-the-art
dance theatre in Lincoln Center) was under construction. The New York
City Ballet was housed at City Center, but Ballet Theatre had no perma-
nent home. Some of the girls in the Ballet Theatre dressing room expressed
the hope that Ballet Theatre could reside at the New York State Theater,

but Lincoln Center was not merely about the arts. It was also about the business, real estate, and political interests of the Old Boys' Network. Lincoln Kirstein was intimately involved with Lincoln Center, and Kirstein was backing Balanchine. Kirstein's longtime friend Philip Johnson was the architect for the New York State Theater, and there were rumors that Balanchine had been consulted about the design.

American dance had always been friendly to women because dance was a low-paying profession of outsiders, but Lincoln Kirstein, the Rockefeller Foundation, the Ford Foundation, and Lincoln Center were merging dance and big business, and the faces of American big business were white, heterosexual men. In the 1950s and 1960s, most of the company directors and choreographers of classical ballet, such as Lucia Chase, Rebekah Harkness, Jerome Robbins, Agnes de Mille, Antony Tudor, and Robert Joffrey, were women or gay men. Robbins had the added baggage of having been a Communist who had testified before the House Un-American Activities Committee. George Balanchine was the choreographer/ballet master who most resembled civic and corporate leaders, and Balanchine had a lifestyle that captured the zeitgeist.

During the 1950s (the initial era of the television show *Mad Men*), *Playboy Magazine* was a cultural phenomenon, and in the early 1960s, Playboy clubs were some of the most popular nightclubs in the country. Balanchine's many ballerina wives and muses were a constant source of gossip and publicity. People couldn't even agree on whether Balanchine had had four wives or five. (Some people counted Alexandra Danilova as a common-law wife, and some people didn't.)

At a time when "good girls" had sex only with their husbands and every state in the union had laws targeting homosexuals, Balanchine glamorized and capitalized on his sexuality in a way women and gay men could not. In the two decades after World War II, Balanchine was placed in a perfect storm of patriotism and the *Playboy* mentality.

In 1962, the New York City Ballet was the company on the rise, but I wasn't a fan of the plotless Balanchine ballets. I wanted to dance the nineteenth-century classics and the twentieth-century ballets of Jerome Robbins, Frederick Ashton, and Agnes de Mille—ballets that illuminated the human condition and had roles for real people with human emotions. Doris Hering's review of the New York City Ballet's fall season in *Dance Magazine* had reinforced my image of the NYCB as a company that produced dancers on an assembly line, ate them up, and spat them out. Hering wrote that the corps de ballet at NYCB had a high turnover rate, that when dancers were first given roles they were mechanical, and that by the time they had the life experience to interpret ballets, they were pretty much finished. She wrote that "with Balanchine, one begins to burn out at thirty." This was not the career I wanted for myself.

In the spring of 1962, I heard rumors that if Balanchine's company moved into the New York State Theater, Ballet Theatre might be forced to relocate to Washington, D.C.—a move which ABT did in fact announce before the end of the year. Ballet Theatre didn't offer the stability I wanted with my parents soon to be four thousand miles from New York.

Ballet Russe, like Ballet Theatre, performed the repertoire I wanted to dance, but Ballet Russe didn't have a tour lined up for the 1962–63 season. If Ballet Russe had no tour, not only would the company not be hiring new dancers, but the current Ballet Russe dancers might be unemployed and auditioning for Ballet Theatre.

On the other hand, if I went to Europe, I could audition for three world-class companies: the Royal Ballet, the London Festival Ballet, and the Paris Opera Ballet. Even the Royal Danish Ballet might be a prospect if I studied at the school during the summer, dyed my hair blonde, and learned the Bournonville style. I knew that at least three of these companies (all but the London Festival Ballet) were funded by their governments and were in no danger of going bankrupt. The stability of the European companies was attractive at a time of turmoil in America.

The other big attraction in Europe was Margot Fonteyn, the dancer I most wanted to emulate. To clinch my choice of the Royal Ballet as the company I wanted to join, the April 1962 edition of *Dance Magazine* included an ebullient photograph of Madame Pereyaslavec hugging Rudolf Nureyev and an article stating that Nureyev wanted to join the Royal Ballet permanently if the technical problems of his citizenship could be worked out. Since Nureyev was a superstar, I had no doubt that the problems would be worked out. The combination of Margot Fonteyn and Rudolf Nureyev made the Royal Ballet irresistible.

The other thing I had to consider was the possibility that no company would want to hire me. If I stayed in New York, I might become like the girl in Madame Perey's class who seemed so talented and accomplished but wasn't in a company. If my family were climbing the Matterhorn, strolling through the Louvre, and watching the Paris Opera Ballet, I might become a bitter little prune if I stayed in New York.

However, if I went to Europe, I could go to England to audition for the Royal Ballet, and I would at least see the Changing of the Guard and Westminster Abbey. If I auditioned for the Paris Opera Ballet, I would see the Arc de Triomphe and the Eiffel Tower, and if I ended up in college, at least it would be the Sorbonne. My French was fluent, thanks to my excellent teachers at Tatnall and the Professional Children's School. A few days after Mom's announcement, I told her that I wanted to travel to Switzerland with the family and join a ballet company in England or France.

I could see that Mom was excited when she wrote that she was selling the house and the cars, that Twink had a piano recital in two days and hadn't even *learned* his music, much less memorized it, and that Dad had arrived safely in Geneva, but before we sailed to Europe, I had two events on my calendar in New York: the Ballet Theatre School demonstration and my high school graduation. The demonstration was the Ballet Theatre School's version of a recital. In the first half of the program, students performed class by class, starting with the least advanced and ending with the most advanced: the Intermediate II class. In the second half of the program, selected dancers from Intermediate II performed divertissements from *Coppélia*. Diana Weber danced the lead role of Swanhilda and was partnered by Richard Beaty, a member of Ballet Theatre. The girls playing Swanhilda's friends included Sharon, Rosie, and me. Fernand Nault, the ballet master of Ballet Theatre, and Madame Pereyaslavec staged *Coppélia* together.

During our final rehearsals on the stage of the Fashion Institute of Technology, Mr. Nault and Madame Perey decided to change the direction of one sequence so that Diana could perform to her better side. (Most dancers do steps better to one side than to the other, and sometimes choreographers allow a soloist to choose her better side.) The problem was that Swanhilda's friends were doing the sequence with her, and most of the girls, including me, preferred the step as originally choreographed and wanted to perform to *our* better side. The question was: should we lobby Madame Pereyaslavec to change back to the original version? I wrote to Mom, and she gave me this advice: "Please dance as best you can, but please don't bother about all the politics and intrigue. Above all, keep your mouth shut!!" She pointed out that these kinds of problems arise in every performance, but since I had always been the star, I hadn't noticed them. Mom wrote that the star always gets preference and that when I joined a ballet company, I would have the same relationship with the prima ballerina that I now had with Diana. Someday, she assured me, I would be the one that others had to accommodate. I relayed Mom's advice to the other girls, and we all agreed to keep our mouths shut and perform as best we could. By the night of the performance, we all knew that Diana was joining Ballet Theatre, and from what I could see, she was a delightful Swanhilda.

The Professional Children's School graduation took place at Hunter College. Dad was in Switzerland, but Mom and my brothers drove up from Wilmington and attended the ceremony. Mom bought me a new dress with a crinoline stick-out slip and a new hat. I also wore nylons instead of bobby socks to look as old as possible. Celeste Holm, an Oscar-winning actress for *Gentleman's Agreement*, handed out the diplomas, and Mom told me afterwards that I practically grabbed my diploma and ran.

The PCS graduation ceremony included a talent show, and I overheard two girls discussing the mother of a pianist named Marvin. "His mother thinks he's God's gift to music," said one of the girls. "If she had *her* way, he'd play *first and last*." I looked at my program and saw that a pianist named Marvin was playing somewhere in the middle—not in the more prestigious positions of first or last. The gossiping girls may have concluded that Marvin's mother had overestimated his talent because he wasn't playing first or last, but many factors go into performance order. Marvin was performing a medley of four songs he had composed for PCS shows—one during each year of high school. No matter how good, a medley of four unknown songs is not the best way to open or close a school variety show in which other students are performing classics in their fields. Time would tell if Marvin had the talent his mother thought he had.

Fourteen years later, in 1976, I was rehearsing *A Chorus Line* at City Center, and Marvin Hamlisch, the composer of the show, mentioned that he had graduated from the Professional Children's School. That night after rehearsal, I located my graduation program and saw that Marvin Hamlisch was the pianist who had played in the middle of the program, and that he was in my graduating class of thirty-two students. Marvin's mother had a good ear. Before his death in 2012, Marvin had won an Emmy, a Grammy, an Oscar, a Golden Globe, a Tony, and a Pulitzer Prize.

As a farewell to America, I went to a beauty salon for the first time and had my hair cut short into a fashionable bubble cut. Most ballet students had long hair pulled back into buns, but I had noticed that some company members had short hair. For class, they didn't have to waste time putting up their hair. For performances, they wore wigs provided by the company. I thought that shorter hair would give me an older, more sophisticated look and would make me appear less like a student and more like a professional dancer. Judging from photographs before and after the haircut, my bubble cut had the desired effect. The new mature me was ready to dance in Europe.

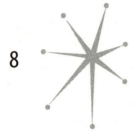

8　Rosella Hightower, Cannes, and Monte Carlo, 1962

The low resonant sound of the ship's horn announced the departure of the S.S. *United States* from New York harbor. Mom, Dad, Trick, Twink, Tuck, and I stood at the railing of the top deck as the ship began to move. People around us threw confetti and streamers and popped corks on champagne bottles. On the docks, hordes of people waved at us, and we waved back. As I stood on the deck and looked at the country I was leaving behind, I didn't anticipate the obstacles ahead, nor did I know that the summer of 1962 would be the most difficult summer of my life.

The transatlantic crossing, however, was a delight. The ship was still inching its way through New York harbor when the maître d' of the first-class dining room led my family to a round table for six and introduced the waiter who would serve us on the five-day trip. I opened the menu, and my heart sang. There were no prices. I confirmed with Dad that food was included in the cost of the voyage, and for the first time in my life, I could eat anything I wanted. And for the next five days, I did.

Some nights, I had avocado vinaigrette, a rare and expensive treat in Delaware. One evening, I had two pineapple sundaes, and by the time the ship docked in Le Havre, I had discovered two new desserts that were worthy of the gods on Mount Olympus: baked Alaska and petits fours. Baked Alaska was a sheet of warm pound cake, topped with a block of cold Neapolitan ice cream, frosted with meringue, which was set on fire to toast the meringue and create a visual spectacle. Baked Alaska had to be ordered twenty-four hours in advance, and I would have ordered it every night, but Mom said that one special request per trip was enough, so I moved on to petits fours, "bite-sized" cakes with unbelievably good frosting.

The S.S. *United States* was a floating city with a movie theatre, a library, and a daily newspaper. Every evening, the passengers dressed for dinner. For the captain's dinner, the most formal event of the voyage, I wore my first little black dress—cotton, jewel-neck, and sleeveless. On board the ship, I felt like a princess, but when we arrived in Switzerland, I turned into a pumpkin.

The house Dad rented in Carouge, a suburb of Geneva, was a mansion compared to our old house in Delaware. All four bedrooms had French doors leading to private balconies, and the master bedroom had its own bathroom. When Dad drove into the driveway, Trick jumped out of the car, ran into the house, cased the four bedrooms, and claimed the best bedroom after the master for himself. Twink and Tuck claimed the other two bedrooms.

"What about me?" I asked.

"You won't be living here," said Mom. "You can bunk in with Twink or Tuck until you join a ballet company."

I hated the idea of rooming with an eight- or ten-year-old boy, especially since Twink and Tuck had eight o'clock bedtimes, so I wandered down to the basement and found an area with four walls and a door. It didn't have any windows or heat, and at the top of one wall, there was a hole about a foot in diameter leading to the backyard. However, in the basement, I thought I would have some privacy. I was wrong. Trick brought home a Swiss girlfriend whose mother traveled much of the time, and Mom moved another bed into the room and told me how good it would be for our family's language skills to have a French-speaking girl living in our home.

I was desperate to take class, but couldn't find a single dance school that was open in the summer. I convinced Mom to drive me to the opera house, but all of the doors were locked, and there was no indication that anyone would be there until the start of the next season in September.

I tried to stay in shape by swimming for the Geneva swim team and doing an occasional barre in my room, but there was nowhere I could really dance. I had always had light, infrequent periods, but suddenly I was gushing blood and getting painful cramps. I didn't know that women who engage in vigorous exercise usually have shorter, less painful periods than sedentary women and that as soon as I started dancing again, the problem would disappear. I had nightmares about dancing in a white tutu and gushing blood in every arabesque.

Mom finally got permission from Dad for me to call the Royal Ballet School from his office. With a script of the anticipated conversation in my hand, I made the call, but the conversation didn't go according to the script. A British-accented voice on the telephone informed me that *if* I could pass the examinations, I could study at the school, but the Royal Ballet could not take foreigners into the company unless they were artists of outstanding merit: stars. I asked if there were a similar rule for the Paris Opera Ballet, and she said she believed there was. The first and only American ballerina in the Paris Opera Ballet was Marjorie Tallchief, and she had become a star before joining the company. I didn't even ask about the Royal Danish Ballet because I had noted in New York that all of the names in that company were Danish. My prospects in Europe looked bleak.

However, before leaving New York, I had asked Madame Pereyaslavec if she could recommend a few ballet teachers in Europe. She had conferred with Mr. Nault and had given me a list with five names: in London, there were the Phyllis Bedells School of Ballet and the Espinosa School. In Paris, there were Madame Preobrajenska and Madame Nora, who taught at Salle Wacker. In Cannes, there was Rosella Hightower at Le Gallia. The only name on the list that I recognized was Olga Preobrajenska.

In her book, *Theatre Street*, Tamara Karsavina wrote that when she first joined the Kirov Ballet at the turn of the twentieth century she particularly admired Preobrajenska. I calculated that Olga Preobrajenska had to be almost a hundred years old. In fact, she was ninety-one and still teaching.

If I couldn't join a company, I could at least study with one of the teachers on the list during the school year. Then, the following summer, when the DuPont company would pay my way home, I could return to New York. I would be a year older, seventeen, and I would be in direct competition with Rosie, but with luck, Ballet Theatre would get an infusion of money and would need several new young dancers.

I thought my chance to find a teacher had arrived when Mom announced that we were going to Paris for a few days. I told her that I wanted to visit Madame Preobrajenska and Madame Nora, but Mom was adamant. "This trip isn't about you. The boys don't want to spend their time looking at ballet schools. We're going to Paris to see Paris." And that's what we did. We went from one tourist attraction to the next, and then we drove to Chartres.

The sight of the Cathedral of Chartres seemingly rising from a wheat field was spectacular, but with every passing hour I felt as if I had less and less control of my life. It didn't help that Trick delighted in stating that the reason that Switzerland was so clean, safe, and efficient was that the men in Switzerland kept women in their place and didn't allow them to vote—a right Swiss women finally won in 1971. Years earlier, Dad had told me with the same twinkle in his eye that the only reason there was a woman in the Senate (Margaret Chase Smith) was that her constituents were too dumb to notice that her husband had died and thought they were voting for him. Both Trick and Dad were joking, but the effect was the same: to remind me that men ruled the world and that no matter how hard I worked, no matter how accomplished I became, I would never be part of the powerful in-group into which they were born.

Mom must have known how unhappy I was that summer, but she was furnishing a house, enrolling Trick at the International School, and learning the rules of living in a foreign country. Two months is nothing to a woman relocating with four children, but to a teenager who is eager to begin her career and is separated from her passion, it is an eternity. The tension between

Mom and me was growing. One day, Mom informed me that as long as I was living in her house, I could at least do some work. While she was out, she wanted me to scrub the kitchen floor.

"What do I use to clean it?" I asked.

"Elbow grease," she said as she left.

I didn't recall seeing elbow grease, but I knew that Mom kept cleaning materials under the kitchen sink. I rooted around, but couldn't find it. I looked under the bathroom sinks. No elbow grease. I checked the cellar. No elbow grease. I looked for "elbow grease" in the English-French dictionary, but it wasn't there.

When Mom returned, she was furious. "You haven't scrubbed the floor!" she yelled. "What have you been doing all this time?!"

I yelled back: "I have searched this entire house from top to bottom, and there is no elbow grease!"

Mom stared at me in disbelief, and then burst out laughing. She mimed scrubbing and said, "elbow grease." I took advantage of the détente.

"Mom," I said, "you didn't give me ballet lessons for twelve years so that I could scrub floors. No one is going to hire a sixteen-year-old dancer they haven't seen. I have to get out of Switzerland."

"You're right," said Mom. "I can't drive to London, and I've been to Paris, so we're going to Cannes. I want to see the Riviera before it gets cold. If you think you might want to stay in Cannes, you should draw up a budget with enough money to survive and *not one cent more*. We'll go from there."

I drew up a truly *survival* budget: a cheap room, ballet classes, toe shoes, basic sundries, and food. I asked Mom if I could add money for clothes or entertainment, but Mom said no. My survival budget was approved by Dad.

I packed two suitcases. I didn't know where I would live, and I didn't know anything about Rosella Hightower, but I did know that I wasn't going back to Switzerland. I had worked for over ten years to escape the suburbs of a city where DuPont wives catered to DuPont executives. I was not going to be trapped in the suburbs of a country where women couldn't even vote.

The resort city of Cannes was the jewel in the crown of the French Riviera. Luxury hotels, including the Carlton and the Martinez, overlooked a sandy beach with open-air restaurants under umbrellas on the sand. Yachts of the rich and famous filled the port, and the Cannes Film Festival was the most glamorous film festival in the world. Cannes had a casino, nightclubs, and palm trees along the Promenade de la Croisette (the beautiful walkway along the beach), but all I wanted to see was Rosella Hightower and the Centre de Danse Classique.

We drove into town from the fragrant city of Grasse, world famous for its perfumes. I wanted to go directly to the Centre de Danse, but Mom wanted to see the Mediterranean Sea. The beaches were not as wide or as white as the beaches on the East Coast of the United States, but the sea was a beautiful blue. Mom and the boys were hungry, so we found a cafeteria where the boys ate at an excruciatingly slow pace. Finally, Mom announced that we had to find a hotel so that the boys could watch television while Mom and I visited the Centre de Danse.

By the time we left the hotel, it was after five-thirty. Fortunately, everything in Cannes was within a few miles, and we quickly found the Centre de Danse, which was located in Le Residence Gallia, a large white building overlooking the city. The entrance to the ballet school was on the left side of the building as we faced it, and when Mom and I entered, we heard voices above us and saw a flight of stairs going up. To our left was a corridor with doors on both sides and no sign of life.

We went upstairs and found ourselves in a large room with tables and chairs and a bar with barstools. This was the *cantine*, where meals were served three times a day, and beverages were available between meals. Mom asked the server at the bar (who was also the cook) about ballet classes, and the server introduced us to Rosella Hightower, who was seated at the bar. Madame Rosella, as everyone called her, was an unassuming woman in her early forties who wore a leotard, hand-knitted wool tights, and no make-up. Her lightly tanned face hinted at her Choctaw heritage. She had the straightforward demeanor of a Midwestern high school principal, but she spoke English with an unfamiliar accent and French with an American accent.

I introduced myself and told her that I had studied at the Ballet Theatre School and that Madame Pereyaslavec and Fernand Nault had recommended her classes.

"How old are you?" asked Madame Rosella.

"I'm sixteen, but I've finished high school," I said.

"Bravo," said Madame Rosella. "What month were you born?"

"January," I said.

"Like me," she said.

How quickly she found something we had in common.

"What day of the month?" she asked.

"The twenty-third," I said.

"Ah," she said. "You're *verseau*."

"*Verseau*?" I asked.

"Aquarius. It's a good sign. Smart. Forward-thinking. *Et tu parles français*?"

"*Oui*," I said because I did speak French.

I was intrigued by the way Madame Rosella jumped back and forth between English and French, but it would be only a few months before I did the same thing whenever I was speaking to someone who spoke both languages.

"I founded the school in the past year," she said, "so it is just beginning. It gives young dancers both dance and *académiques*. I also want the Centre to become a meeting place for professionals. They can *détendre* (relax), take class, exchange ideas, and go to the *plage* (beach)."

Madame Rosella's goal sounded ambitious, but not yet achieved, and I had reservations about a school where everyone came to relax.

"I'm teaching the six o'clock class this evening," she said. "If you brought a leotard, you should take it. Jacqueline can show you around later. She's in charge of the rooms downstairs if you want to live at the Centre."

"I'm really out of shape," I said. "I haven't danced all summer."

"That doesn't matter," she said. "I'll be able to see what you can do."

She was so sure of herself that all of my insecurities vanished.

After changing into my leotard, I entered the largest studio I had ever seen. It had numerous, open windows, and the studio was much cooler than Madame Pereyaslavec's hotbox at Ballet Theatre. Unlike Madame Pereyaslavec, Madame Rosella did not make a grand entrance. When she walked into the studio, students continued to stretch and chatter among themselves, but when Madame Rosella clapped her hands, there was immediate silence. She demonstrated the pliés, and the class began.

To my surprise, I didn't feel out of shape at all. I knew I'd be sore the next morning, but I was so energized to be back in class that I danced quite well. I saw Madame Rosella's approval when I did pirouettes and saw her reservations when I jumped. I couldn't tell how good a dancer she was—or had been—because when she demonstrated combinations, she didn't dance full-out. She didn't try to impress anyone. She simply conveyed what she wanted us to do. In my first class, it was her intelligence that impressed me. She seemed to know exactly what each student required.

As I watched the other dancers, I thought that I compared favorably, but I knew that professional dancers usually take class in the morning before their rehearsals and performances—not in the evening. Even on vacation or between engagements, professionals stick to their morning regimen.

During Madame Rosella's class, I saw that the dancers had many different styles. Some were Russian-trained; others Cecchetti-trained, and still others danced in a looser style, which I later recognized as French. In the 1950s and 1960s, dancers were divided as to how far hips should deviate from the horizontal in pursuit of higher extensions. Some dancers, especially the English, thought that lifting the hips was vulgar; others, especially the French, thought that freedom in the hips was modern and exciting. I leaned toward the English stance for pragmatic reasons. I didn't have a particularly high extension, so I liked to think that this was because I, like Margot Fonteyn, kept my hips under control, but I'm sure that if someone had proved to me that I could have raised my legs an additional ten or twenty degrees by raising my hips, I would have come down firmly in the camp of the French.

Madame Rosella did not impose a particular style on the class, but gave corrections to improve whatever style the dancer already had. If I studied with her, I could maintain my Russian technique and also experiment with new ideas.

After class, I told Madame Rosella that I wanted to stay in Cannes and study with her.

"Good," she said. "Marika Besobrasova in Monte Carlo and I are putting together a performance to celebrate Prince Rainier's birthday on November 19th. I'd like you to take part in the program."

I had no idea what the program might be, but I told Madame Rosella that I'd love to be a part of it. In Cannes, I wasn't in a company—or even in a city with a company—but I had escaped the suburbs of Geneva, and by working with Rosella Hightower, I could grow as an artist.

After I changed back into my street clothes, Jacqueline, a tall young French woman, showed Mom and me the living accommodations on the ground floor. Jacqueline told me that the rooms were designed for two people, but since the Centre wasn't full, Madame Rosella had said that I could have a double room to myself until they needed the space. The rooms were Spartan with two single beds, two desks, two armoires, and a sink with running water. No one would come to the Centre de Danse to be pampered.

Jacqueline wasn't just in charge of the rooms, she also supervised the children who lived and boarded at the Centre, took them to a local school for academic studies, and taught History of the Dance. I knew that Mom was relieved that she could tell Dad that I was living in a school with supervision and an American in charge.

After Mom left, I unpacked my suitcases and set out to explore the rest of the building. At the end of the hall was a closet-size room with a toilet. In a nearby room, there was a bathtub. A sign above the tub indicated that baths cost four francs, only one franc less than a ballet class, so I would have to shower in the communal showers upstairs by the girls' dressing room. As I exited the room with the bathtub, two young girls came out of a nearby room and introduced themselves. Martine was twelve; Maryse was eleven, and the two sisters shared a double room with their mother who was always perfectly dressed from head to toe. Martine and Maryse were a fountain of information, and I asked them to please correct me when I made errors in French.

"You don't make many errors," said Martine, "but sometimes you sound a little like a book—very formal."

"I'd rather be too formal than too familiar," I said.

"Yes," Martine agreed, "and there's one word you shouldn't ever say: the m-word."

"It's not polite," said Maryse.

"The m-word?" I asked.

"It's what you see in the toilet … brown," said Martine.

My French teachers at Tatnall and PCS had neglected to teach me that word.

Martine whispered in my ear, "*Merde*. You must never use that word except before a performance."

I didn't understand what Martine was trying to tell me, but I knew to be on the lookout for *merde*, and soon, I understood three functions of the word. Its literal translation is "shit." *Merde* is also used as a swear word, but on the power scale, it is more equivalent to "damn" than "shit." It is also the word dancers use to wish each other luck before a performance. Just as American actors say "break a leg," and opera singers say *in bocca al lupo* (in the mouth of the wolf), French dancers and dancers from many other countries say *merde*.

Martine and Maryse were flabbergasted that I had never heard of Rosella Hightower and informed me that Madame Rosella was a huge star. She had been *première étoile* (first star) with the Grand Ballet du Marquis de Cuevas (de Cuevas Ballet) and had recently given a series of performances with Rudolf Nureyev. In fact, I would soon learn that Rosella Hightower was as well known in France as Margot Fonteyn was in England.

In the summer of 1961, after Rudolf Nureyev defected from the Soviet Union, he joined the de Cuevas Ballet, and Rosella Hightower was one of his most frequent partners. When Fonteyn invited Nureyev to make his English debut at a charity event in London, Nureyev chose Hightower to be his partner, and their *Black Swan Pas de Deux* created a sensation. The Grand Ballet du Marquis de Cuevas disbanded in 1962, the year after the Marquis died and only a couple of months before I arrived in Cannes, but Rosella Hightower, Sonia Arova, Rudolf Nureyev, and Erik Bruhn joined together and gave a series of all-star performances. This unassuming American teacher with whom I had taken class that evening was a bona fide star. Her plan for the Centre de Danse, which had seemed so ambitious a few hours earlier, now seemed exponentially more attainable.

Rehearsals for Prince Rainier's gala were held in the big studio of the Centre de Danse and in Marika Besobrasova's studio in Monte Carlo. Madame Rosella and Marika Besobrasova seemed to be friends as well as colleagues, and the rehearsals were exactly what I imagined when I contemplated a career in dance. The choreographers knew what they wanted, stated or demonstrated what they wanted, and helped the dancers achieve the desired effect. I was cast in three ballets: *La Péri* (choreography by Juan Corelli), *Médée* (choreography by Juan Corelli), and the evening's closer, *Scènes de Ballet pour une Fête Nationale* (Ballet Scenes for a National Celebration), a new ballet to be choreographed by Rosella Hightower and Marika Besobrasova.

In *La Péri*, a young man goes in search of the Flower of Immortality, which is held by a mythological creature called the Péri. The young man steals the flower, but the Péri enchants him with her dancing and retrieves the flower, so the young man dies. Rosella Hightower was dancing the Péri, and André Prokovsky, the role of the young man.

Médée is based on the Euripides play about a woman who kills her children when her husband Jason leaves her for a woman of higher birth. Rosella Hightower was dancing Medea, and Stefan Grebel, Jason. The other two characters in the ballet were the children Medea strangles, and I played one of the two.

Scènes de Ballet pour une Fête Nationale was a ballet with exotic birds at court, and I was one of three *oiseaux gris* (grey birds). One of the girls in this ballet, a member of a company in Germany, disappeared during rehearsals, and I was given the small solo which had been choreographed for her.

There are three routes between Cannes and Monte Carlo: the Basse Corniche, the Haute Corniche, and the Moyenne Corniche. All three roads are cut into the seaside cliffs, and the higher ones have hairpin turns and spectacular views. The Basse Corniche is the coastal route, which is usually jammed with tourists. The Haute Corniche is the highest route with a bird's eye view of the cities below. The Moyenne Corniche is the middle route, which was considered to be the most efficient route. This was the road we traveled.

I was one of three dancers assigned to the Citroen DS driven by Jean

Robier, a theatre designer who designed some of the sets and costumes for this performance and who was married to Rosella Hightower. Monsieur Robier referred to his car as the "DS" (pronounced "Day-ess"), and I assumed he was calling the car a goddess, because *déesse*, the French word for "goddess," is pronounced almost the same as DS. The name was appropriate. The Citroen DS was a sleek, cutting-edge car, which held the road like a mountain goat. Today, the Citroen DS is probably best known as the classic car actor Simon Baker drives in the television show, *The Mentalist*.

This commute to Monte Carlo was my real introduction to French drivers. On the Moyenne Corniche, drivers honked once to announce their intention to career around hairpin curves, straddling the center line, at Grand Prix speeds. Drivers hearing a honk were expected to hug the mountain or the edge of the cliff to let the honking car pass. I didn't want to think about what might happen if cars in both directions honked simultaneously and both straddled the center line.

I would soon learn that French drivers treat traffic laws as minor inconveniences established to challenge their ingenuity. Once, on my way to the Nice airport in a car *not* driven by anyone connected to the Centre de Danse, I was in the back seat when the car barreled through a red light without slowing down. My eyebrows flew up into my hairline as I looked at the driver's pre-teen daughter sitting beside me. Sensing my concern, she said chidingly, "Papa, that was a red light."

"Ah, yes," he said, "it was red *then*. But if we'd waited for it, it would have turned *green*."

Voilà! The French approach to driving.

I was relieved when we arrived safely in Monte Carlo and parked outside the casino, which looked like a large luxury hotel. The theatre was inside the casino, and I looked forward to seeing the gaming rooms where I imagined that all of the men wore tuxedos and all of the women wore Schiaparelli or Givenchy. However, because I was a minor, I was stopped at the door. A member of the casino staff escorted me to a back entrance, and this was the entrance I had to use while the other dancers went through the main entrance and saw the world-famous casino.

Years later, when I finally had a chance to visit the casino, I was surprised at how poorly some of the men were dressed—even men gambling serious money. Jackets were required, so the atmosphere was not as casual as in Las Vegas, but some of the men wore jackets that didn't match their pants, and some wore suits that were ill-fitting and rumpled.

My disappointment at not seeing the interior of the casino evaporated when I saw the ornate red and gold theatre designed by Charles Garnier, the architect of the Paris Opera House. This intimate but spectacular Monte Carlo theatre seated about five hundred people, and from the stage, the large royal box high above the orchestra seats dominated the view.

Rehearsals for the gala culminated in the tech, orchestra, and dress rehearsals. One of the dancers told me that in the de Cuevas Ballet, dancers were not permitted to eat, drink, smoke, or sit down when they were in costume, and although I didn't know if these rules applied to this performance, I obeyed them because I thought they made sense.

The tech (technical) rehearsal is an onstage rehearsal with sets and lights, and dancers usually don't perform full-out in this rehearsal because they use the rehearsal to accumulate information. During the tech rehearsal, I looked to see exactly how the curtains were hung to delineate the wings and made sure to exit on the same angle so that I wouldn't hit the curtains. If the curtains are disturbed—even by a tutu in the wings—they will ripple and create a distraction on stage. I noted how much of the stage was lit at any given moment and made sure that my counterpart on the other side of the stage and I used the same reference points to find our positions so that we didn't have to watch each other during the performance to be symmetrical. This was familiar territory because of my performances with Mr. Jamieson and the Ballet Theatre School.

My costumes were all dance-friendly, and I listened carefully to the orchestra, not only for tempos, but also for the orchestrations, because a movement performed to a single violin has a different value from a movement performed to the blaring of trumpets.

Finally, it was November 19th, Prince Rainier's birthday. Shortly before the performance, I put on my toe shoes and went upstairs from the corps de ballet dressing room to get the feel of the stage. I peered through a peephole in the curtain to look at the glamorous audience and saw the two empty seats where Prince Rainier and Princess Grace would take their places immediately before the performance. I still had the opening ballet, *Pas de Quatre*, to finish my make-up and put on my costume.

Monsieur Robier had given a couple of make-up lessons at the Centre to show the new girls how to apply stage make-up, but since I had never used make-up off stage, I needed more time than most of the other dancers. When my make-up was as perfect as I could make it without false eyelashes, which I couldn't afford and which Monsieur Robier had assured me were the least necessary part of make-up because eyelashes don't read past the first few rows, I changed into my costume for *La Péri*, put rosin on the interior of the heels of my toe shoes, and then put the heels under running water so that they would stick to my tights.

Between entrances in *La Péri*, I watched the ballet from the wings, and Rosella Hightower was a revelation. This middle-aged teacher, wife, and mother of a seven-year-old turned into a siren on stage. Her performance was electric. Until this moment, the star dancers I had seen had all been charismatic off stage. Maria Tallchief had a regal, commanding presence that was impossible to miss, and Margot Fonteyn was a perfect little jewel, but offstage, Rosella Hightower looked like an ordinary person. Her transformation was fascinating.

The third ballet of the evening was the Minkus *Pas de Trois*, with choreography by George Balanchine performed by Anita Kristina, Yélé Kernic, and André Prokovsky. Anita, who had danced Taglioni in *Pas de Quatre* earlier in the evening, was a tall dancer who was movie-star beautiful. In the summer, she wore very short shorts, and men would stop dead in their tracks to stare at her.

The fourth ballet was *Médée*, followed by *Pas Classique Espagnole* from *Le Cid*, which was choreographed by Julien Calderon and performed by Rosella Hightower and Juan Guiliano. The evening came to a close with *Scènes de Ballet pour une Fête Nationale*, a ballet in four scenes which involved the entire company. Prince Rainier, Princess Grace, and their guests gave us an enthusiastic ovation.

Back in the dressing room, I was getting out of my costume when someone in the hall called out, "The Prince and Princess want to meet the dancers on stage."

"Get out of your costume first," said my dresser, and I obeyed. My mind was racing. No one had taught me how to greet a prince and princess. Should I curtsey, shake hands, or bow? Should I speak only when spoken to? I saw that all of the other dancers, still in costume, were on their way upstairs followed by the dressers, including mine. I was wearing only tights, trunks, and toe shoes. I couldn't get back into my costume by myself, because it was so snug that I had to hold it tightly around my waist while my dresser pulled up the long zipper in the back. My dressing gown was stained with make-up, and my street clothes made me look like a schoolgirl. I didn't want to embarrass the company, so I decided to stay in the dressing room and prayed that no one would notice my absence. As the minutes passed, I began to pack up my make-up. Then I realized that if my make-up were packed up when the other dancers returned, they would know that I hadn't gone upstairs, so I unpacked my make-up and put it back exactly where it had been.

When I heard voices coming back downstairs, I went into the toilet. I waited until it sounded as if most of the dancers and dressers had returned. Then, I came out of the toilet, washed my hands, and began to pack up my make-up again. If the other dancers noticed my absence, they didn't mention it. I hoped I would get another chance to meet the Prince and Princess, but I never did.

However, by the end of the evening, I had met all the choreographers who had attended the gala: Anton Dolin, Juan Corelli, and Julien Calderon, in addition to Madame Rosella and Marika Besobrasova. The only choreographer who had not attended the gala was George Balanchine. Outside the casino, everybody kissed everybody goodbye, but there was no sadness because the dance world is small, and we all expected to see each other again. In my hands I held my souvenir program, which was white with the royal seal in gold. Inside the program, Madame Rosella had written: "To my Lee, *fille adopté* [sic] (adopted daughter)."

Reverend Joseph D. C. Wilson and President Franklin Delano Roosevelt with Secret Service.

Mom and Dad on their wedding day.

Age six, in my
birthday cake
recital costume.

With Trick, in our mushroom costumes.

Valentina Pereyaslavec and Rudolf Nureyev, 1962. Martha Swope © The New York Public Library.

Rosella Hightower, Jean Robier, and Bigoudi in the *cantine* at the Centre de Danse, 1962.

In schoolgirl clothes and a bubble cut hairdo on my bed at the Centre, 1962.

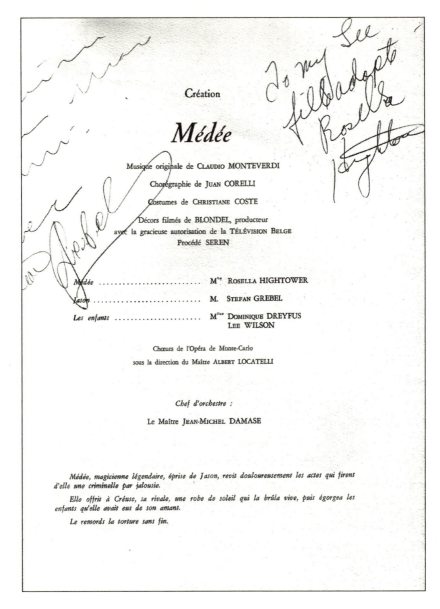

Création

Médée

Musique originale de CLAUDIO MONTEVERDI

Chorégraphie de JUAN CORELLI

Costumes de CHRISTIANE COSTE

Décors filmés de BLONDEL, producteur
avec la gracieuse autorisation de la TÉLÉVISION BELGE
Procédé SEREN

Médée	Mlle ROSELLA HIGHTOWER
Jason	M. STEFAN GREBEL
Les enfants	Mlles DOMINIQUE DREYFUS
	LEE WILSON

Chœurs de l'Opéra de Monte-Carlo

sous la direction du Maître ALBERT LOCATELLI

Chef d'orchestre :

Le Maître JEAN-MICHEL DAMASE

    Médée, magicienne légendaire, éprise de Jason, revit douloureusemens les actes qui firent d'elle une criminelle par jalousie.

    Elle offrit à Créuse, sa rivale, une robe de soleil qui la brûla vive, puis égorgea les enfants qu'elle avait eus de son amant.

    Le remords la torture sans fin.

Program page from the Command Performance in Monte Carlo, with autographs of Rosella Hightower and Stefan Grebel, 1962.

Taking class at the Centre de Danse with Maina Gielgud and Alfonso Cata, c. 1963. Courtesy of Maina Gielgud.

Rosella Hightower and André Prokovsky in *Black Swan Pas de Deux*, 1964. Photo by Arks Smith, Harvard Theatre Collection (bMS Thr 450 [19-2]), Houghton Library, Harvard University.

Erik Bruhn, 1968. Photo by Arks Smith, Harvard Theatre Collection (bMS Thr 450 [114]), Houghton Library, Harvard University.

Margot Fonteyn and Rudolf Nureyev in *Swan Lake*, 1965. Photo by Arks Smith, Harvard Theatre Collection (bMS Thr 450 [51]), Houghton Library, Harvard University.

9 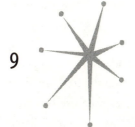 Bruhn, Nureyev, and Paris, 1963

I had made my professional debut, but for the rest of the winter, I was in limbo. I wasn't a child who went to school during the day, but I wasn't a peer of the older dancers who had performed with ballet companies and visited Cannes for a few days or a few weeks and were more likely to stay in small hotels than at the Centre. In New York, I had had a concrete goal: to graduate high school and join Ballet Theatre. In Cannes, I had no idea where or how I might join a company. However, I was improving and expanding my technique, learning from the vast array of dancers I saw in class, and working on a daily basis with an artist whose opinions were respected throughout the dance world.

Two teachers besides Rosella Hightower helped establish the Centre de Danse: José Ferran and Arlette Castagnier. José (pronounced "Zho-zay") was the perfect counterpart to Madame Rosella. He was dedicated, direct, even-tempered, and gave an excellent class. He alternated with Madame Rosella in teaching the morning and evening classes, and when he taught,

Madame Rosella often took the class. Arlette, who had previously danced with the de Cuevas Ballet, taught the children's classes.

José also taught Spanish dance, which required a different posture from classical ballet. In classical ballet, the back is straight and the butt is minimized, but in Spanish dance, the posture accentuates the crescent curve of the back. All of the students in the class were girls, so once we knew the steps, José moved around the room dancing opposite each girl.

When Madame Rosella took class, she sometimes worked on only one part of her body for the entire class—her feet, her arms, or her head. By focusing on only one thing myself, I became more aware of exactly what I was doing at each moment, and I discovered new ways of performing the movements.

Madame Rosella had exceptionally high jumps, and she often prepared for them with four or five running steps in plié, not with the traditional up and down movements of a *chassé*. I had seen Russian men use this running approach, but not women. The approach wasn't classical, but Madame Rosella's jumps were explosive, and they appeared even higher because she kept her body low to the ground before the jump.

One day, when teaching class, she shouted at me, "*Sautez! Sautez!* Jump!"

I jumped as high as I could, but Madame Rosella clapped her hands and stopped the music. "I want you to run like a football player," she said. "I don't care how you look. Just get off the ground. Let me see."

I did my imitation of a football player, ran full speed ahead, and jumped with as much power as I could muster.

"Better," she said. "Do that for the next two weeks."

Madame Rosella was asking me to do with my jumps what I had previously done with my spins—focus on the climax and then refine the preparation. For the next two weeks, I ran like a football player before every jump. I could feel that my elevation was better, and in subsequent weeks, I worked to incorporate the higher jump into my technique by alternating *chassés* with runs in plié. I knew that I'd need pretty *chassés* for nineteenth-century classical ballets, but I could use the running approach for modern ballets. I felt less comfortable in class because I had to think about every approach, but my leaps were higher.

Twenty-five years later, I was vacationing in Cannes and took Madame Rosella's class while a dancer friend of mine watched. Madame Rosella, her hair by then white, demonstrated the big jumps, and my friend's jaw dropped in astonishment. At age sixty-eight, Rosella Hightower was still jumping as high as the men.

My life in the studio was inspiring, but my life outside of the studio was limited by my lack of money. My main meal of the day was *café complet* at the *cantine* in the morning. *Café complet* was a large cup of half milk and half coffee with lots of freshly baked bread, butter, and jam. I still needed to lose a few pounds, so Monsieur Robier advised me to eat a small breakfast and then have protein and salad for lunch, but I couldn't afford protein and salad every day. However, once or twice a week, I walked to a lovely little restaurant called L'Omelette, which had the lightest, fluffiest omelets I had ever tasted with a choice of glorious golden French fries or a salad with a perfectly balanced vinaigrette dressing. The tastiest, most substantial omelet was *omelette au jambon* with large chunks of ham, but the least expensive and the least caloric was the *omelette fines herbes* (fresh herbs), so I usually had the *fines herbes*. Once or twice a month, I splurged for a meal with meat.

Shortly after I arrived at the Centre, Carlos Carvajal, an American who had been a soloist with the de Cuevas Ballet, asked me what I thought about the situation in Cuba. Since I didn't have access to radio, television, or newspapers, I had to admit that I knew nothing about it. Carlos told me that I had a responsibility to know what my country was doing and informed me that Russia had installed missiles in Cuba, and President Kennedy had issued an ultimatum to Premier Khrushchev. I hurried to a bookstore to learn more.

"*Bonjour, mademoiselle, bonjour,*" said the proprietor as I entered the shop.

"*Bonjour, madame,*" I said.

"How can I help you?" she asked.

"I'm just looking," I said, and when I saw the disappointment in her eyes, I wanted to sink into the floor.

The French, unlike Americans, don't go shopping to entertain themselves. When a French woman enters a store, she usually intends to buy something, and since French shoppers are loyal to their chosen bookseller, butcher, baker, and even bank teller, every new person who walks into a shop gives the proprietor an opportunity to form a new, long-term relationship. But I had nothing to offer this proprietor. I was a thief who was stealing information by reading the front page of the *International Herald Tribune* without paying for it. I was embarrassed that I couldn't afford a newspaper, but I was even more embarrassed to look like a fool in front of Carlos. Carlos was smart, well-educated, and well-traveled. Madame Rosella joked that when they were both touring with the de Cuevas Ballet, the boat would dock, Carlos would disappear, and by the end of the day, Carlos would be fluent in the local language.

In the bookstore, I read that American U-2 planes had flown over Cuba and had identified offensive missile sites. President John F. Kennedy had informed the nation that he would search ships bound for Cuba and would turn back ships with offensive weapons on board. He had also demanded that Russian Premier Khrushchev halt and eliminate the build-up in Cuba. Many people believed that the world was on the brink of war.

Switzerland had been neutral during both World Wars, and my parents had a bomb shelter in their backyard in Geneva, but if I returned to Geneva, I might get trapped in Switzerland, and the fear of being trapped far from a ballet class outweighed the fear that I might be in a different country from my parents during World War III. A few days later, I was relieved to hear that Khrushchev had agreed to dismantle the sites in Cuba in return for Kennedy's assurance that the United States would never invade Cuba.

I had no money to buy warm tights for the cold studio, but Françoise Parlier, one of the French dancers who had performed in Prince Rainier's gala, came to my rescue. After she was given new wool tights for Christmas, she lent me her heavy cotton ones for as long as I remained at the Centre. Martine and Maryse gave me scissors, thread, and a needle whenever I needed to sew ribbons on toe shoes, which wasn't often compared to other dancers. For most of my life, Mom had expected me to wear toe shoes until I outgrew them, so I was accustomed to wearing very soft shoes. I hated the clonking sound of new toe shoes, so I never wore new shoes on stage—only in class and rehearsals. When the shoes were well broken in and no longer made noise, I placed them in rotation with my older shoes. Later, when a company was buying my shoes, I put new shoes under a faucet, filled the boxes with water, dumped out the water, and put the shoes on my feet so that they would soften and conform to my feet more quickly, but I still rotated shoes and wore them for months.

One Sunday, Madame Rosella invited me to spend the afternoon with her and several other people in St-Paul-de-Vence, a charming medieval town in the inland mountains between Cannes and Nice. It was wonderful to get further from the Centre than my own two feet could take me, and I loved spending the day with Madame Rosella. As we walked around St-Paul-de-Vence, Madame Rosella pointed out the spectacular views and identified the colorful flowers. She was one of the most efficient people I ever met, but she took time to enjoy life. She told me about dinner parties with exotic dishes I had only heard about, like paella and couscous. She said that coffee made her sneeze, but she wouldn't give it up because she liked it too much. As we wandered through the scenic town, she told me that she had American citizenship by birth and French citizenship by marriage, and that when she was pregnant, she returned to the United States so that her daughter Monet would be born there and would also have dual citizenship.

Monet often came to the Centre after school, and sometimes, Martine, Maryse, Monet and I played cards. When there was a snowstorm and all of the schools suspended classes to let the children play in the snow, Monet and I built a snowman almost five feet tall.

The other member of the Robier family was a curly white poodle, Bigoudi (hair curler), who sometimes watched class from under the piano. Like Jillana's Tiger, Bigoudi would sit up during the applause after class. When class was dismissed, Madame Rosella sometimes took off a ballet slipper and threw it across the room. Bigoudi snatched it, and Madame Rosella chased the fluffy white ball of fur around the studio. When playtime was over, Madame Rosella clapped her hands, and Bigoudi brought her the shoe.

In January of 1963, Madame Rosella performed in Paris and wrote that she was working with a very talented young dancer, Attilio Labis of the Paris Opera Ballet, and was bringing him to Cannes in February so that we could see him. The following month, Rosella Hightower, Attilio Labis, and five other dancers performed half a dozen ballets including the *Black Swan Pas de Deux*.

Madame Rosella's Black Swan was very different from Margot Fonteyn's. Fonteyn had a vulnerability which not only fooled the Prince into believing that she was the girl he had fallen in love with, but also suggested that her father might have forced her to impersonate Odette. Rosella Hightower, on the other hand, was a fireball of sexuality—a woman confident of her ability to seduce and dazzle the Prince. Even if the Prince had suspected that she was an imposter, he wouldn't have been able to resist her. Hightower breezed through the technical challenge of the fouettés and did two and a half or three and a half turns *à la seconde* instead of the usual one and a half.

A third distinctive interpretation of the Black Swan was that of Maya Plisetskaya, prima ballerina assoluta of the Bolshoi Ballet. Plisetskaya was a force of nature—every inch her father's daughter. Instead of fouettés, she did a demonic circle of piqué turns.

Swan Lake's music and choreography are passionate, tender, and exciting, but part of the reason that the ballet is so popular is that the role of Odette/Odile can support many different interpretations. Odette can be a vulnerable young girl who has fallen victim to a supernatural power, or she can be a passionate woman fighting for her life, who knows that the Prince is her only chance for freedom. Love can be the Achilles heel that dooms the Prince as well as Odette, or it can be the saving grace which allows both to transcend death. The ballet can be a tragedy when the protagonists die, or transcendent when they overcome death and are united in a better world. The themes are universal and timeless. What is the relationship between humans and the supernatural? What is the power of love?

Madame Rosella's performances at the casino theatre with Attilio Labis were followed by a program with eight stars of the Paris Opera Ballet. The following month, Zizi Jeanmaire, a singer as well as a dancer, arrived with her company of forty in her Music-Hall show. I loved seeing so much high-quality dance, but the cost of tickets was decimating my budget, and the fact that I was sitting in the audience underscored the fact that I had turned seventeen and was still not in a company.

My frustration with my lack of money and mobility was exacerbated when Mom came to Cannes to have lunch with a sorority sister who was taking a cruise of the Mediterranean. This was the first time I had ever seen Mom travel alone or have lunch with someone outside of the family. The minute Mom saw me, she criticized my hair. I explained that I had to wash it with bar soap because I couldn't afford shampoo, and that I cut it with borrowed paper scissors, but Mom made it clear that my lack of funds was my problem, not hers.

At lunch, as I listened to Mom talk with her sorority sister, I could see that she had redefined her life in Switzerland, and she seemed happier than I had ever seen her. She was driving around Europe with Twink and Tuck and was seeing the great art and architecture that she had previously seen only in books.

On our way home from lunch, Mom gave me the news of the family: Dad had moved into the basement bedroom because he had back pain and needed a board under his mattress, so Mom was getting the first good sleep she had had in fifteen years because Dad was no longer kicking her in his sleep. Trick was zipping around Geneva on his new red motorcycle, would travel from Russia to Spain, and would score a perfect 800 on his college boards while Twink and Tuck were skiing the mountains of Switzerland and France. It was wonderful to hear news of the family, but I couldn't help noticing that everyone in my family was traveling except me. I asked Mom why she didn't answer the letters I addressed to her and Dad, and she said, "That's not my job anymore. It's your father's." Mom had taken me from Wilmington to Philadelphia to New York to Geneva to Cannes, but for the next step, I was on my own.

Today, young dancers can go on the internet and research companies, salaries, unions, and auditions. Websites like www.answers4dancers.com are packed with information. For example, under "salaries," dancers can compare minimum salaries of Broadway shows, national tours, cruise ships, and theme parks. The site also lists upcoming dance auditions and provides advice and exposure for dancers. In the United States today, there are numerous dance competitions such as Youth America Grand Prix, the USA International Ballet Competition, and the Spotlight Awards, which can all be researched online. But in the early 1960s in France, dancers communicated in person, by telephone, or through letters and telegrams. Long distance telephone calls were expensive, and there were no public telephones at the Centre. For the one call I made to my parents that year, I walked to the post office, waited in line, gave an employee the number I wanted to reach, and waited in the designated booth until the call was connected.

In the United States, the major ballet companies and their schools were all within walking distance of each other in New York, but in France, the opera ballet companies were scattered around the country (Bordeaux and Marseilles were probably the best-known outside of Paris). In addition to the opera companies, there were two important French choreographers, Roland Petit and Maurice Béjart. Roland Petit, based in Paris, choreographed ballets, films, and the popular Music-Hall show for his wife, Zizi Jeanmaire. Maurice Béjart, based in Brussels, had an avant-garde company, Ballet du XXe Siècle (Ballet of the Twentieth Century). European countries had work laws concerning foreigners and minors, but I didn't know what they were or how to find out about them. I had no idea how I might begin a career in Europe.

I wasn't traveling the world that winter, but I was seeing it from a different point of view. In the United States, I had learned that American boys liberated Paris at the end of World War II. In France, I learned about the pregnant girls they left behind. In restaurants, I could barely hear French voices at the next table, but I could hear Americans across the room. In the United States, wounded veterans marched in Veterans' Day parades. In France, the damage was not only in the bodies of men, but also in the walls of buildings and the bones of children who couldn't get enough milk during the war.

I learned that good manners in one country may be poor manners in another, and that in France, I should keep both hands on or above the table during meals. I learned that although *mal au coeur* begins with the word for "ache" or "pain" and ends with "heart," the phrase doesn't mean "heartache" or "pain in the heart," but "sick to the stomach." I learned that it's embarrassing to confuse *collants* and *culottes* (tights and panties).

Americans strove for "life, liberty, and the pursuit of happiness," goals of the individual. The French strove for *liberté, égalité, fraternité* (liberty, equality, fraternity), goals of the society. In France, education, health care, and the arts were all considered too important to be left to private enterprise and were subsidized by the government. In France, the biggest event of the year was not the religious celebration and consumer bonanza of Christmas, but *la rentrée*, the children's return to school in the fall and the adults' return to work after summer vacations. Compared to Americans, the French focused less on the accumulation of money and material goods and more on the quality of their lives and personal relationships. Life was less comfortable in France, but more egalitarian.

The winter of my discontent became a spring of joy when Madame Rosella told me that Erik Bruhn was coming to Cannes to teach us the second act of *La Sylphide* for two performances at the casino theatre. When Erik Bruhn arrived, he arrived with Rudolf Nureyev. These two men were the most sought-after male dancers in Europe, and they were a study in contrast. Bruhn was cool perfection; Nureyev was passion personified. When Bruhn entered the studio, every blond hair was in place, and his practice clothes looked as if they might have been ironed. When Nureyev entered the studio, his dark hair was tousled, and his practice clothes were rumpled. The atmosphere was electric when the two men were working together.

Bruhn was scheduled to dance both performances, but while he was teaching us the choreography, Nureyev stood in for him and danced with Madame Rosella. All three stars marked most of the steps until the performance, and during the next few months, I was impressed with how easily the lead dancers changed partners. The contrasting styles of Bruhn and Nureyev in *La Sylphide* illustrated the fact that even if one dancer is the acknowledged master of a particular role (as Bruhn was with *La Sylphide*), another dancer can bring a different quality and give a performance that has its own value. Bruhn and Nureyev were polar opposites, but both were compelling.

I had admired Erik Bruhn ever since I was a pre-teen ballet student in Wilmington, and during the year that I was studying with Madame Pereyaslavec, the sexual heat he generated in Ballet Theatre's production of *Miss Julie* had been the talk of New York. Because of his elegant look and bearing, I had assumed that he was tall, but when he walked into the studio in Cannes for the morning class, I saw that he was only about five feet seven.

Height and weight on stage can be deceiving. When I was dancing in *A Chorus Line*, many people who came backstage were surprised at how short and thin the dancers looked up close. In fact, Baayork Lee was so petite she made everyone else look tall, and the overhead lighting accentuated our muscles and curves and added pounds to our figures.

During rehearsals for *La Sylphide*, Madame Rosella introduced me to Erik Bruhn and told him that I could translate English to French if he wished me to do so. Bruhn certainly spoke some French, but he seemed more comfortable in English, and he occasionally asked Madame Rosella or me to translate a word or a phrase.

Madame Rosella was dancing the lead role, but there was also a solo danced by Jacqueline de Min, a lovely dancer with clean, effortless beats (legs tapping together in the air, often with quick changes of position). Jacqueline had performed the role of Grisi in *Pas de Quatre* in Monte Carlo and again in the recent performances in Cannes. Madame Rosella told me to learn her solo in *La Sylphide* because it would be a good role for me in the future.

On April 20th, after five months of dancing only in the studio, I was finally back on stage, dancing in the corps de ballet of *La Sylphide*, *La Péri*, and *Raymonda*. The program opened with *Raymonda*, with Anita Kristina and Jimmy Urbain in the lead roles. After *Raymonda*, Claude Bessy and Attilio Labis (both from the Paris Opera Ballet) performed *L'Oiseau des Neiges*, and Rosella Hightower and Erik Bruhn performed the *Flower Festival Pas de Deux*. Following the first intermission, there were two ballets: *La Péri* with Anita Kristina and Jimmy Urbain and *Daphnis et Chloé* with Claude Bessy and Attilio Labis. Ending the evening, after a second intermission, was the second act of *La Sylphide* with Rosella Hightower and Erik Bruhn. For these two performances, I received a salary of one hundred francs, minus a few francs for social security. Out of this, I had to pay fifty francs for costumes for the upcoming recital, which left me with over forty francs, the cost of eight ballet classes or half a dozen meals in a restaurant.

The school recital on April 23rd was every bit as important as the professional performances, because, in the recital, I was dancing solos, and I knew that Madame Rosella and Monsieur Robier (who designed the costumes and was an astute judge of ballet dancers) would be assessing my viability as a soloist. Madame Rosella had given me two contrasting roles: the Finger Fairy variation from *Sleeping Beauty* and a comedic role in *Les Patineurs* (The Skaters). The Finger Fairy variation required speed and precision, but had no big jumps or difficult spins. *Les Patineurs* had flashier movements and a character to play. During rehearsals, I had had reservations about the simplicity of the Finger Fairy variation, but once I was in my yellow tutu, I felt I could sparkle like my costume. And I loved performing in *Les Patineurs*. I loved hearing the audience laugh.

I was still savoring the joy of these three performances when Madame Rosella informed me that an impresario from Paris had seen our opening night and had booked us into the Théâtre des Champs-Elysées in Paris and the Bordeaux Opera House in Bordeaux. I was finally going on tour! It was a mini-tour at the end of May with four performances in each city.

Erik Bruhn left for his next engagement, and Madame Rosella informed me that she was going away for a few days and wanted me to rehearse the corps de ballet in *La Sylphide* while she was gone. I was astonished that she had chosen me, and I have no idea what she told the other girls, but they were all very supportive when I told them that rather than running the ballet from start to finish, I wanted to stop and start to ensure that we all moved at the same speed, through the same positions, with our legs at the same height. When Madame Rosella returned, she told us that our unison was much better, which it was.

I was excited about dancing in Paris, but not particularly excited about seeing the city, which I had visited twice before. The first time was a one-night stopover on the way from Le Havre (where the S.S. *United States* docked) to our new home in Geneva. The second time was when Mom packed the children in the car and I wasn't allowed to visit the ballet schools. On the first occasion, the weather was cold and rainy, and I was very sleepy because I had stayed up until midnight to celebrate our last night on the ship. When we checked into the hotel in Paris, I told Mom that I wanted to take a nap, but she said, "I told you to go to bed *early*. You're in Paris, and you're going to see Paris." She herded the entire family into a tour bus to see the landmarks of the City of Light. My brain was so foggy and the sound system was so poor that I couldn't figure out if the guide was speaking English or French, and the landmarks, when viewed through a rain-spattered window, seemed far less interesting than they appeared in books. On the second trip, I had enjoyed the paintings and sculptures in the Louvre, but the rest of the city seemed congested and dirty.

Seeing Paris from the point of view of a professional dancer was a completely different experience. With one other dancer, I shared a large hotel room with a balcony overlooking a scenic street. Every morning, as soon as I woke, I went out onto the balcony to breathe the fresh air and see the action in the street. Then I rang for a *café complet*, which was served in my room. The company had chosen the hotel, and I didn't know how much it cost or who was paying for it, but I trusted Madame Rosella to make sure that whatever I was being paid would cover my expenses, which it did with money to spare. Outside of rehearsals and performances, I could do exactly as I pleased.

I walked the length of the Champs-Elysées from the Louvre to the Arc de Triomphe. At the beginning of the walk, the Arc de Triomphe was a small arch in the distance, but as I walked closer, it loomed larger and larger until I felt like an ant awed by the huge edifice before me. I enjoyed a magnificent ice cream sundae at Le Drugstore, a fashionable restaurant that had distinctive gold and white matchbooks for patrons who smoked, as most French adults did. Madame Rosella took several of us to the Louvre, and then we stopped by a studio where Zizi Jeanmaire and Roland Petit were rehearsing, and Madame Rosella introduced us. After our performances, we dined in elegant cafés. This was the way I wanted to live my life. This experience was light years away from traveling with Mom.

The performances in Paris and Bordeaux were billed as the Hommage au Marquis de Cuevas, a tribute to the deceased Marquis de Cuevas by some of the stars of his company. We used the sets and costumes of the de Cuevas Ballet and performed some of its repertoire.

The very theatrical Marquis de Cuevas was born in Chile, married a granddaughter of John D. Rockefeller, became an American citizen, and established his ballet company in the mid-1940s. In the late 1950s, the Marquis, age seventy-two, and dancer/choreographer Serge Lifar, twenty years younger, made headlines when they engaged in a duel over the staging of a ballet. Duels were illegal, but the press was invited, and there is even video of the duel-ending moment when the Marquis nicked the arm of Lifar and drew blood.

The Grand Ballet du Marquis de Cuevas disbanded in 1962, a year after the death of the Marquis and shortly before I arrived in Europe. Many people spoke of the de Cuevas Ballet as a golden age in French ballet.

The British dance critic Clement Crisp wrote in the April 2005 edition of *Dance Research* that "*Le Grand Ballet du Marquis de Cuevas* was a delight to ballet-goers. It possessed that most precious of attributes, theatrical glamour. Its performances seemed always to have a frisson of excitement to them. It was rich in star dancers, artists who thrilled by their bravura as by their emotional command over their roles . . . you breathed a theatrical ozone more heady, more intoxicating, than the quieter airs inhaled during the usual run of dutiful performance on home ground, or even with such visiting luminaries as New York City Ballet and American Ballet Theatre."

In the Hommage au Marquis de Cuevas in Paris and Bordeaux, the stars included Rosella Hightower, Marjorie Tallchief, Genia Melikova, Liane Daydé, André Prokovsky, Nicholas Polajenko, Vladimir Skouratoff, and Michel Renault.

For me, the greatest challenge of this engagement was the raked stage of the Théâtre des Champs-Elysées. When I first stepped onto the stage, I felt as if I might skid to the footlights and tumble into the orchestra pit. I had read that many Russian and European stages were raked, and this was one of them. The back of the stage, near the backdrop, was higher than the front of the stage, near the orchestra and the audience. (This is why the back of the stage is called upstage, and the front of the stage is called downstage—whether or not the stage is raked.) A raked stage offers challenges that a flat stage does not. On a flat stage, gravity pulls a dancer straight down toward the ground. On a raked stage, gravity pulls a dancer forward and down. If a dancer is in profile to the audience, she is pulled to one side. If a dancer has to perform a manège, a series of turns in a circle, she must work harder on the first half of the circle to push herself uphill. Then, as she hits the upstage point of the circle, she must put on the brakes for the second half of the circle to avoid spinning out of control. Nevertheless, she must make each turn look identical and effortless. I was glad I was in the corps de ballet and didn't have to perform thirty-two fouettés on a rake.

Three days before we opened in Paris, *Suite en Blanc* was taken off the program and replaced by a pas de deux from *Roméo et Juliette*. The male lead was changed in *Aubade*. I wrote to Mom that I had never seen "so much confusion, switching, unreadiness, and general disorder in my life." Nevertheless, the opening night in Paris, with Maria Tallchief in the audience, was a big success.

Between rehearsals and performances, I took class with four different teachers: Serge Peretti, Madame Illich, Mischa Resnikov, and Madame Nora. Serge Peretti taught the stars of the Paris Opera Ballet and was inscrutable. Madame Illich told Stefan Grebel that I had given her students "a good lesson." Mischa Resnikov addressed me as "Baby American" and corrected every move I made. Madame Nora confirmed that Madame Rosella's "football" approach to jumps had been a success when she said I should have told her about my jumps so she could have put me in the group with the boys. At a dinner party after our last performance, a couple of the stars congratulated me on my "success in the studios." News traveled fast in the French dance community, and by taking class with four different teachers, I had raised my profile in the company.

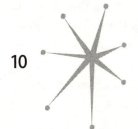

10 Maina Gielgud, *Pas de Quatre*, and Vichy, 1963

When the Hommage au Marquis de Cuevas arrived in Bordeaux, the press met us at the train station, and photographs of the company were on the front pages of the newspaper for the next two days. The caption on one of the photos was *Pluie d'étoiles* (Rain of stars), and the photo showed the female members of the company reaching for the pom-poms on the hats of French sailors. I didn't know why we were told to reach for the pom-poms, but someone said it was a French tradition.

When we got to our small hotel, Madame Rosella paired me with Maina Gielgud, who, in Paris, had stayed at her mother's apartment. I had met Maina at the Centre de Danse, and she had danced with us when we performed at the casino in Cannes, but I didn't know her well because she always stayed in a hotel, and I was awed by the fact that she was the niece of one of England's greatest actors, Sir John Gielgud. Maina was tall, with long black hair, and had already danced with Roland Petit's company and with the de Cuevas Ballet. I guessed that Maina was in her early twenties, and I admired the talent, technique, dedication, and intelligence that would make her a principal dancer with the London Festival Ballet and later, director of the Australian Ballet and the Royal Danish Ballet. In Paris, Maina was one of the dancers Madame Rosella had invited to the Louvre, and Maina had been very helpful in directing me to the ballet teachers in Paris. At the Centre, Maina often came to class with two male dancers, and I wondered if one was her boyfriend, or if she might be so sophisticated that she had *two* boyfriends at the same time.

The moment Madame Rosella announced that Maina and I would share a room, Maina said, "No. I need a single room." Realizing that she might have offended me, she said, "It's nothing personal. I always room alone." However, the small hotel was completely booked, so Maina agreed to double up for one night.

The desk clerk asked about our breakfast orders. Did we want croissants or rolls?

"Both," said Maina and I in unison.

We looked at each other in surprise.

"Jam or butter?" asked the desk clerk.

"Both," said Maina and I in unison.

As we unpacked, I learned that Maina was only eighteen, one year older than I, but she had grown up bilingual and knew all of the biggest stars in French ballet while I was still cocooned in the suburbs of Delaware. I asked her if one of the two male dancers with whom she came to class was her boyfriend, and she laughed out loud. "No, no," she said, "the two boys are a couple. They've been together for ages."

I had read about homosexuals and would later realize I had worked with and admired quite a few, but this was the first time I had heard anyone state that a person I knew was gay. Unlike people in Delaware who blushed when they described Liberace as "light in his loafers," Maina wasn't the least bit embarrassed to identify her friends as gay. Her direct statement is typical for the dance community where sexuality is openly discussed, the majority of male dancers are gay, and people do not discriminate based on race, creed, nationality, or sexual orientation. (Governments, unions, and other organizations may discriminate, but the dancers themselves generally do not.)

As Maina and I unpacked, I learned that we had a lot in common. We both idolized Madame Rosella. We both had complicated relationships with our mothers, and we were both dedicated to becoming the best dancers we could be. Maina was a combination of the person I was, and the person I wanted to be, and she quickly became my best friend.

The Bordeaux press gave us a warm reception and positive reviews, but the audiences were reserved. The stars were not greeted with applause on their entrances the way they had been in Paris, and the only really enthusiastic reception was for the *Black Swan Pas de Deux* danced by Madame Rosella and André Prokovsky.

I took two classes with the Bordeaux Opera Ballet. The ballet master gave good, solid classes, but I was uncomfortable in the studio, which had a 4 percent slope, just like the stage. In Paris, classes had been a series of performances. In Bordeaux, they were work that had to be done.

After the final performance, there was a farewell dinner party, followed by a tour of *les caves*, the cellars of a winery that specialized in the dessert wines Sauternes and Barsac. I didn't drink alcohol, but I loved watching the other dancers perform the ritual of wine tasting: admiring the color, sniffing the bouquet, sipping the wine, bouncing it over the taste buds, and then spitting it into buckets so as not to get drunk. The tour ended at 4:00 AM, and our train back to Cannes left two hours later, at 6:00 AM.

During the wine tasting, one of the female dancers announced that she was madly in love with one of the male stars and was going to follow him back to Paris. Madame Rosella pulled me aside and told me she was flying back to Cannes and needed me to take the train ticket for the love-struck dancer and make sure she got on the train. I quickly packed out of my room and went to the other girl's room. I suspected she had done too little spitting and too much swallowing in *les caves* and would re-think her infatuation in a few hours. After she told me about her *grand amour*, I pointed out that since she didn't know exactly where the object of her affection lived, and might not look her best after being up all night, it might be smarter to return to Cannes, get a good night's sleep, and go from there. Fortunately, she agreed. When she was safely on the train, and the train pulled out of the station, I gave her the return ticket.

Maina told me she was leaving our crowded second-class compartment to sneak into an empty first-class compartment where she could stretch out and sleep, and she asked if I wanted to come along. I was afraid the conductor would force us to buy first class tickets, but Maina assured me that we'd have time for a nap before the conductor came by and that he would simply send us back to second class, which is exactly what happened.

The following week, with the money I had earned in Paris and Bordeaux, I bought a pair of black slacks and a gold mesh change purse so that I would look less like a schoolgirl and more like a professional dancer.

Maina's mother, Zita Gielgud, wasn't enthusiastic about Maina's friendship with me. Mrs. Gielgud, a former dancer and a widow, was glamorous and theatrical. She wore make-up, silk scarves, and sunglasses—movie-star sunglasses, not clip-ons like Mom. Maina told me that her mother referred to me as "that American child," and criticized my use of vulgar American words like "mirror" instead of the more refined "looking-glass." Of course, when Maina told me this, I banished "mirror" from my vocabulary for as long as I lived in France. Since Maina looked older than her age and knew the French social rules, I could understand that Mrs. Gielgud might think an American teenager who was just learning the rules might detract from Maina's stature as a future star, and I was impressed that Maina defied her mother to be friends with me.

I envied Maina her sophisticated mother, who was knowledgeable about ballet and was interested in Maina's career, and I think Maina envied me my apparent freedom from a mother who left me alone. Both of our mothers thought their daughters were too fat. Both mothers were better at criticism than praise. "But at least *your* mother stays home," said Maina. "Mine pops up wherever I go. And she stays *forever*." We were both trying to break free from the expectations of our mothers and find our own places in the world.

Many years later, when Maina was director of the Australian Ballet, she told me about her retirement from performing. "I woke up one morning," she said, "and I thought I'd kill myself if I had to dance one more Swan Queen. I couldn't tell Mummy I wanted to retire so I told the press. Mummy read about it in the newspapers. She wasn't pleased. But it was the only way I could make sure I retired." Our mothers were very different, but Maina and I are both products of our mothers' hopes, dreams, and determination.

Once or twice, Maina invited me to join her for tea in the garden of her hotel, which was a short walk from the Centre de Danse. Occasionally, we went to the beach. In the sun, I was careful to cover up from head to toe because I had heard that in some companies, girls were fired if they got suntans. Dancers portraying sylphs (beings who are part air) and Wilis (spirits of brides who were jilted before their wedding day) were expected to have skin so white that under blue light, it looked almost translucent. Once or twice, Madame Rosella, Mrs. Gielgud, Maina, and I went to the beach together, but Maina and I spent most of our time in the studio.

When Madame Rosella was teaching, Maina and I danced in different groups so that we could watch and critique each other. When Madame Rosella took class, we danced in the same group so that we could watch Madame Rosella and discuss what she did. Some afternoons Maina and I pooled our resources and took a semiprivate class with Madame Rosella to work on something specific, such as arabesque turns. Madame Rosella certainly gave us attention in class, but it was very helpful to work for a full hour on one spin or one technical problem. In addition to addressing our weaknesses, these classes strengthened the bond between Maina and me and between each of us and Madame Rosella.

The friendship between Maina and me was cemented when we began to work on *Pas de Quatre*. Anton Dolin, a British dancer who was the foremost authority on *Pas de Quatre*, flew in from London to stage the ballet. We were scheduled to dance three performances in Vichy on three successive weekends, with later performances in Deauville and Besançon.

Mr. Dolin told us that *Pas de Quatre* was created in 1845 as a competitive showcase for the four greatest ballerinas of the time: Marie Taglioni, Lucille Grahn, Carlotta Grisi, and Fanny Cerrito. We would not only dance the choreography of *Pas de Quatre*, but would also portray these four ballerinas as they were in 1845. Taglioni was the greatest star of her time and intended to show her superiority in this ballet. Taglioni would be danced by Rosella Hightower. Grahn was a younger ballerina who was nipping at the heels of Taglioni and planned to prove that she was Taglioni's equal. Grahn would be danced by Maina Gielgud. Carlotta Grisi was the first ballerina to dance the role of Giselle and was the least competitive of the four ballerinas. She would be danced by Véronique Landory of Les Grands Ballets Canadiens. Fanny Cerrito was the flirt who always checked out the men in the front rows. Cerrito would be danced by me.

I had no idea how to flirt. The closest thing I'd had to a date were the mandatory school dances at Tatnall when I was thirteen and fourteen.

After a few days of feeling woefully inadequate and hopelessly miscast, I asked myself, "Why does Cerrito flirt? What is she trying to accomplish?" And I answered, "She flirts because she wants to make people love her." I could identify with that. How could I make the audience love me? Unlike an actress, who can choose her body movements, such as crossing her legs, a dancer must perform movements already determined by the choreography. But as I analyzed the ballet step by step, I realized that there were moments when I could play peek-a-boo with the audience, and there were times, after a few quick steps, when I could hit a pose as if to say, "Look at meeeeee!" My Cerrito would be a girl who wanted to sparkle and be loved.

Mr. Dolin explained that all four ballerinas were consummate professionals, so the rivalries should be subtle. For example, after the opening variation, which is danced by all four ballerinas, three of the dancers (Taglioni, Grisi, and Cerrito) leave the stage, so that Grahn is left alone for the first solo. However, before leaving the stage, Taglioni hesitates, turns back to Grahn, and gestures to her, thereby stealing the focus and implying that she (Taglioni) is in charge. Grahn graciously acknowledges Taglioni—as if the exchange were part of the original choreography—and acts as if Taglioni's gesture were a gesture of deference. All of this interplay should enrich, but not overpower, the dance.

As Mr. Dolin described the characters, he taught me how to approach a role, which I realized later is similar to the way a journalist approaches a story: by asking who, what, when, where, why, and how. Who am I? What is my function in this ballet? When does it take place? Where does it take place? Why am I doing what I'm doing? And finally, how am I going to convey to the audience and the other dancers what I need to convey?

I worked alone in the studio for hours. I worked on my arms, my legs, and my eyes. I danced my variation slow motion and at breakneck speed. The more different ways I rehearsed, the better I knew what I wanted to do. Then Maina and I worked together. I critiqued her as she danced her variation, and she critiqued me as I danced mine. Then, she asked me to perform her variation.

"I can't carry off a *grande dame*," I said.

"That doesn't matter," said Maina. "You might do something I can use— or something that gives me an idea."

So I danced her variation, and, in fact, she saw a couple of things she wanted to play around with to see if they worked for her. Then I asked her to dance my variation. "I can't," she said. "I'd feel silly. I'm not little and cute like you are." This comment was a turning point in my comfort level in the role. I knew in principle that some roles were better suited to young dancers than others, but it hadn't occurred to me that Cerrito might be one of them—that my youth and energy might add a different color to the palette of the ballet. I also realized that *Pas de Quatre* had two advantages for me over some other ballets. First, the skirts were mid-calf length, which would cover my muscular thighs. Second, the ballet was a nineteenth-century period piece, and I knew from looking at Degas paintings that many nineteenth-century dancers had curvaceous figures. By the time we left for Vichy, I was feeling reasonably confident of my ability to play Cerrito.

Vichy was known as La Reine des Villes-D'eaux (The Queen of the Water Cities). There were springs in the middle of the city where people lined up to buy a fixed amount of mineral water at fixed times to cure whatever ailed them. The water was supposed to cure everything from poor digestion to irritated skin to arthritis. Vichy water was used internally, by drinking it, or externally, by taking thermal baths. There were even octagonal pastilles made from minerals distilled from the water. The pace in Vichy was leisurely, with elegantly dressed visitors filling the streets, the spas, and the theatres. The city was particularly fashionable in the summer during the arts festival at the casino.

We arrived in Vichy late at night, checked into the hotel, and got a short night's sleep. The next morning, we walked from the hotel to the theatre and saw posters four feet tall announcing the Hommage au Marquis de Cuevas. I was thrilled to see my name on the poster and noticed that Maina's name was misspelled—as it often was in programs—but Maina didn't seem to mind. Her focus was on the work, not the publicity, and we had a long day ahead: costume fittings and orchestra rehearsal in the morning, dress rehearsal in the afternoon, the performance at 9:00 PM, and the long drive home.

The four ballerinas in *Pas de Quatre* wear identical costumes (although their hairstyles are different), and I was given the smallest costume. As I stepped into the pink skirt, I saw the name on the waistband: Alicia Markova. I was stepping into history. Alicia Markova was a British ballerina who was a star in the 1930s and 1940s and was often partnered by Anton Dolin. In 1947, on the opening night of Ballet Russe at the Metropolitan Opera House, Markova was scheduled to dance *Giselle*. However, she became ill, and a younger ballerina, Rosella Hightower, danced the role for the first time and captivated the audience and the critics. I was stepping into a costume which Alicia Markova had worn, and I would soon be dancing with Rosella Hightower. For a seventeen-year-old girl with a love of history, it doesn't get better than that.

In the first half of the program, I danced in the corps de ballet of *La Sylphide* and *Aubade*, which gave me time to get the feel of the stage and the audience. *Pas de Quatre* was the first ballet after the intermission, or the interval, as I now called it in the hope of winning points with Maina's mother. Madame Rosella took her opening position, and the other three of us took our positions around her. The curtain rose, and the familiar music began. All four of us danced the opening variation. I had seen the way Madame Rosella used her eyes to great effect when working with her partners, but when she looked at me, in full make-up, I was still surprised by the focus and the intensity of her gaze. I could see the challenge in her eyes daring me to be better than she was, and I was determined to meet her challenge. When we both danced toward our spots splitting center stage, there was laughter in her eyes as she could see me making sure that she wasn't closer to center than I. In what seemed to be a nanosecond, the ballet was over. We had all danced our solos. We had performed the final variation for all four dancers, and now it was time for the curtain calls. Maina was first. Véronique was second. I was third. As I came offstage, Maina looked at me in shock. "Did you hear the applause?" she asked. I hadn't heard anything. As Madame Rosella took her solo bow, Maina whispered, "You got more applause than Madame Rosella." I felt sick. I hoped Maina was wrong or that Madame Rosella hadn't heard the applause. I didn't want to be Eve in *All About Eve*. I planted a smile on my face and followed Maina on stage for the group bows, which seemed interminable. Finally, the curtain fell, and I heard Madame Rosella's jubilant voice, "Did you hear?! Did you hear the applause?!" And then she was hugging me.

I wasn't the only young dancer who had had a success that evening. Maina was asked to stay in Vichy to rehearse and perform one of the lead roles in the Walpurgis Night Ballet in the opera *Faust*, which was scheduled for the following Friday night. I made a hotel reservation so that I could come up by train Friday morning, see Maina's performance, and get a good night's sleep before our second performance in Vichy.

I loved performing with the Hommage au Marquis de Cuevas. I was dancing a classical repertoire, working with great artists, and having experiences I would never have had as a tourist. But I wasn't dancing every night, and I wasn't earning a living. In January, I would turn eighteen, and I didn't know if my father would continue to support me. I needed a full-time job, but I was trying to launch my career at a very difficult time.

In the United States, the two great touring companies, Ballet Russe and Ballet Theatre, seemed close to death. Ballet Russe was in its last season, and Ballet Theatre, which had made an unsuccessful move to Washington, D.C., was limping back to New York. In Europe, the de Cuevas Ballet had disbanded in the summer of 1962, and many of the dancers, from the stars to the corps de ballet, were still looking for jobs. Madame Rosella, who was in her early forties and had founded the Centre de Danse, might not want to perform full-time, but some of the other stars were a decade younger, and Maina was obviously a future star. If these dancers were doing sporadic performances with the Hommage au Marquis de Cuevas, it seemed unlikely that I could do better. With no touring company in continental Europe, the Paris Opera Ballet restricted to the French, and the Royal Ballet reserved for the British, I didn't know where I might fit in. But Madame Rosella did.

When we returned to Cannes after my first *Pas de Quatre*, Madame Rosella called me into her office and told me that I had been offered the position of *première danseuse* (first dancer) of the Bordeaux Opera Ballet. This was the number three position in the second most prestigious company in France. The two girls above me were the *première étoile* (first star) and the *deuxième étoile* (second star). I would be dancing important roles in operas, operettas, and ballets. Carlos Carvajal, the American dancer who had told me about the Cuban missile crisis, was the new assistant ballet master and male *deuxième étoile*. Jens Graff, a young Norwegian dancer who had recently visited the Centre, was the new *premier danseur* and would be my partner. Madame Rosella said that the contract would begin on October 1st and that it was time for me to get out of the studio and onto the stage. If I accepted the contract, Madame Rosella would ask Carlos to find me a place to live prior to my arrival in Bordeaux. The salary was one thousand French francs a month.

One thousand francs was one hundred and fifty francs more than Dad was sending me in Cannes, and in Bordeaux, my ballet classes, which were currently my second biggest expense after rent, would be free. Jens Graff was a good young dancer so this was an excellent job.

On Friday morning, I took the train to Vichy to see Maina perform in *Faust*. This was the first full-length opera I had ever seen, and I was enthralled. The voices were wonderful; the sets were fantastic, and the story about a man who sells his soul to the devil had me on the edge of my seat. The Walpurgis Night Ballet took place in the realm of the devil, and Maina was very good, but the ballet didn't begin to show what she could do.

The following night, I danced my second *Pas de Quatre* and received my first bravos. After the performance, Madame Rosella told the company that everyone in town had seen our program, so we had to change it. In our third performance, we would dance the second act of *Giselle* and the second act of *Swan Lake*. The Vichy Opera Ballet, which knew both ballets, would supply the corps de ballet. Beatrice Mosena, the ballet mistress of that company, asked Maina and me to stay in Vichy that week so that Maina could rehearse the role of Myrtha, the Queen of the Wilis in *Giselle*, and I could learn one of the four little swans in *Swan Lake*. Maina and I both signed guest artist contracts.

The week in Vichy was delightful. I liked living in a new city and dancing with a new company of dancers. The London Festival Ballet was in town, so I took their company class. After class, I told the ballet mistress that I had been offered the position of *première danseuse* in Bordeaux, but that I had not yet accepted it or seen a contract, and I wondered if the London Festival Ballet might be another option. The ballet mistress said she was sure she could find me a place in the company. I decided to discuss my options with Madame Rosella, but in the meantime, we had our final performance in Vichy.

In the first half of the program, Maina was superb as the Queen of the Wilis. She was strong technically and cold as ice when she refused to spare the Prince's life. Maina had so much authority on stage it was hard to believe she was only eighteen.

The second act of *Swan Lake* ended the evening. In the wings, we four little swans crossed our arms in front of our bodies, took each other's hands, and walked onto the stage in silence. As if we were one body, we took our starting position. The music began. Our feet moved up and down like pistons as we zigzagged back and forth across the stage. Our heads moved at a precise pace, at a precise angle. I could sense the exact height of the legs of the dancer beside me. Unlike *Pas de Quatre* in which four dancers dancing the same steps are all trying to stand out as individuals, in this dance, our goal was to be identical, and judging from the applause and Madame Rosella's nod of approval, we succeeded.

On the drive home to Cannes, we made a short detour for croissants that Madame Rosella said were some of the best in France. We arrived at the bakery before dawn, and the croissants were still warm from the oven. They were crisp and flaky on the outside and soft on the inside. As the pastries melted in our mouths, we all looked at each other in silent satisfaction.

During the time I was performing with the Hommage au Marquis de Cuevas, I don't recall hearing any of the dancers complain about the casting. If there were problems among the ever-changing stars, which in Besançon included Nina Vyroubova and Daphne Dale, the news didn't trickle down to me, and as far as I could tell, the young dancers who were nurtured by Madame Rosella trusted her judgment and didn't question her choices. Our roles and the size of our billing varied from city to city and gave us a sense of where we stood in the hierarchy of the ever-changing company, which had no formal positions.

When we traveled by car, Maina and I jockeyed for position to get into the car driven by Madame Rosella, and we were often successful. Our late-night discussions ranged from dance to personal experiences to religion. Madame Rosella told us about the night she made her entrance as Giselle, tripped on the doorstep of the house, and skidded to the footlights on her butt. She recounted her escapades with Mischa Resnikov, her first husband, and how before their marriage, she once crawled out a window so she wouldn't be caught in his room. She told us that Antony Tudor was a Buddhist, and we talked about the concept of reincarnation. I was fascinated by the idea of past and future lives and bought a set of four little books about the four paths of yoga which lead to god/nirvana/perfection: the paths of love (bhakti yoga), work (karma yoga), knowledge (jnana yoga), and psychological exercise (raja yoga). I thought that dancers had a lot in common with practitioners of karma yoga. Both groups seek perfection through work. Both seek experiences that transcend everyday life. And for both groups, the work itself, not the money earned from the work, is what matters.

Once we were back in Cannes, I told Madame Rosella about the possibility of the London Festival Ballet and asked her advice. She told me that the Festival, and *only* the Festival, was better than Bordeaux. However, every dancer in Europe was trying to get into the Festival, and the competition for roles was fierce. At the Festival, I would be in the corps de ballet. In Bordeaux, I would be dancing important roles. Madame Rosella thought

I should be dancing important roles. But whatever my decision, I had to make it fast.

My decision was Bordeaux, and Madame Rosella said that she would have the company send me a contract. When it arrived, there were six original documents, with the details typed into each one. The contract was on parchment-colored paper and had an insignia and lettering which made it look like an Important Document. The first page stated that Monsieur Roger Lalande, director of the Grand-Théâtre Municipal, was acting on behalf of the mayor in hiring Mademoiselle Wilson. Page two began with my stipulation that I was *majeur* (the age of majority, which in France was twenty-one). I drew a line through that phrase. The duration of the contract was October 1, 1963, to April 30, 1964, "with the possibility of prolongation at the discretion of the management." I certainly wasn't going to sign a contract that could be extended for my entire career, so I added the words, "but no later than June 30, 1964." In my cover letter I explained that a new contract could be signed after that date if we both agreed. In addition to my salary, I would receive seventy francs a month for toe shoes, reimbursement for round-trip travel from Paris (which I changed to Cannes), and reimbursement for two hundred kilos of baggage, which was more than twice the weight of me and everything I owned.

Pages three and four consisted of rules: The management could cancel the contract after my first performance if they didn't like my work. I would have to dance any and all roles that I was assigned. I was exclusive to the Bordeaux Opera House for the duration of the contract and could not dance anywhere else without permission. On performance days, I was required to check the bulletin board no later than noon for matinees and no later than 6:00 PM for evening performances to see if there were any changes. If I were sick and couldn't perform, I would pay for the cost of my replacement or for the cancellation of the performance. This point gave me pause, and I wouldn't agree to it today, but when I was seventeen, it seemed reasonable. No one in the Hommage au Marquis de Cuevas had ever missed a performance, and I was confident that if I were hit by a bus, Carlos and the ballet master would figure out how to replace me or the ballets I was dancing.

Paying another dancer to replace me seemed fair, and it was inconceivable that a performance would be cancelled just because of me.

There was only one rule which seemed odd. Unless I had special permission, I was not allowed to watch performances from the wings or from the house—not even by purchasing a ticket. I could understand that the management wouldn't want extraneous people in the wings, but I couldn't imagine why the theatre wouldn't sell tickets to the dancers. I decided to deal with that provision after I arrived in Bordeaux. I signed all six copies of the contract and sent them to Mom and Dad to cosign. Dad ran them by a French-speaking lawyer for the DuPont company, who made no additional changes and told Dad that I knew what I was doing. I was giddy with delight at having a full-time job, but in the meantime, I would dance in an unforgettable performance in Tipaza, Algeria.

Poster for the Hommage au Marquis de Cuevas with Maina's name misspelled.
Photo by Robert Woods.

Première Danseuse in Bordeaux. Photo by Bonnefon.

Backstage in *Hello, Dolly!*

Arabesque, 1970. Photo by Joan Weaver.

In *Oklahoma!* at the New York State Theater in Lincoln Center, 1969. Photo by
Arks Smith.

As Patty in the original Broadway Company of *You're a Good Man, Charlie Brown,* 1971. Martha Swope/© The New York Public Library.

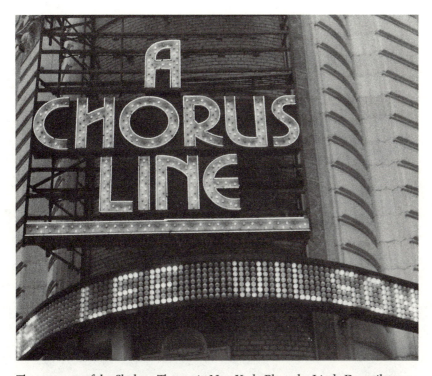

The marquee of the Shubert Theatre in New York. Photo by Linda Dangcil; courtesy of Dick Hamilton. On September 29, 1983, *A Chorus Line* became the longest-running show on Broadway. This record-breaking performance was a black-tie event for an invited audience, which included Helen Hayes, Liza Minnelli, and Mikhail Baryshnikov. There were eight successive casts, beginning with the then-current New York Company, followed by the Original Broadway Company. "Nothing" was performed in Japanese by a dancer from the Japanese Company, and during the Cassie dance, Donna McKechnie was joined by seven additional Cassies. The final scene, the "alternatives scene," was performed in many different languages by a cast chosen from foreign companies, including companies in Sweden, Germany, Australia, and Spain. There was no Kristine from a foreign company, so Michael Bennett asked me to perform the role in French. The stage had to be reinforced to support the more than 330 dancers in the finale. In the week leading up to the record-breaking show, the dancers' names scrolled across the marquee. The publicity from this performance gave new life to the Broadway run.

Wearing the Gypsy Robe on opening night of *Meet Me in St. Louis*, 1989.
Photo by Naomi Naughton.

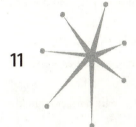

11   Algeria, Naples, and Bordeaux, 1963–1964

The political situation in Algeria was volatile. In July 1962—the month I stepped off the S.S. *United States* onto French soil— Algeria, after more than a hundred and thirty years as a French colony, won its independence from France. During the following months, as fighting continued among factions within the African country, roughly one million French citizens who had settled in Algeria (the Pieds-Noirs) left Algeria and flooded back into France. French newspapers were filled with speculation about how the return of the Pieds-Noirs would affect the French economy and how their departure from Algeria would affect the stability of the African country. Only days before our performance, Ahmed Ben Bella had been elected president of Algeria, and Ben Bella was scheduled to attend our performance as his first public appearance after the election.

On the morning of our flight to Algeria, our passports were still in Paris awaiting visas. Madame Rosella treated this as a minor inconvenience and told everyone to bring their *cartes d'identités* (identity cards) instead. Only two of us—Louise Naughton (an Australian girl who had recently arrived at the Centre) and I—didn't have identity cards. "Never mind," said Madame Rosella, "I'll get you into Algeria on mine."

Louise was a hard-worker and a big fan of Madame Rosella, so for the month of September, Maina, Louise, and I formed a trio. September was bittersweet not only because I was about to leave Madame Rosella and Maina, but also because Madame Rosella, Maina, and some of the other dancers were planning to tour China. I would have loved to go with them, but in 1963, U.S. citizens were forbidden to travel to China. Madame Rosella could risk having her U.S. passport revoked (which it was) because she also had a French passport, but I had only one.

As we flew across the Mediterranean Sea to Algiers, the pilot invited us into the cockpit. We went up in groups of two or three, and when I entered the cockpit, the pilot asked me if I'd like to fly the plane. At first, I thought he was joking, but he wasn't. I declined, but one of the male dancers quickly downed his champagne and took the controls.

When we landed, the immigration officials seemed perplexed that many of us had no passports and that Louise and I had no *cartes d'identités*, but Madame Rosella said that she'd take care of everything and she did. Within minutes, still at the airport, we were at a cocktail reception, and Madame Rosella was giving television interviews. Although the fighting at this time was *within* Algeria—not between France and Algeria—Madame Rosella stressed the fact that we were an *international* company with dancers from America, England, Australia, Switzerland, Hungary, and Italy.

As we were driven to our hotel, I saw that the population in the streets was young and male. Algeria had been a part of many empires—the Carthaginian, Roman, Byzantine, and Ottoman—and for several centuries, the country had harbored the infamous Barbary Pirates—pirates who not only captured European and American ships and demanded ransom, but also invaded the coastal towns in France, Spain, and Italy, kidnapped the inhabitants, and sold them in huge slave markets in Africa. One of the biggest slave markets in the world had been in Algiers.

Our hotel accommodations were beautiful and comfortable. We were told not to unpack our luggage, that the staff would do it while we were at dinner. And what a dinner it was—a banquet with more meat than I had eaten in months, more courses than I could count, and exotic food that was absolutely delicious. After the banquet, Madame Rosella announced that we had to rehearse that evening. The theatre was outdoors, and during the day, the sun would burn us to a crisp.

We were driven to an outdoor Roman amphitheatre with room for two thousand five hundred people. Our raised wooden stage was still under construction, so we had to dance around the missing pieces. In the moonlight, I could almost see the ghosts of Sophocles and Euripides, whose plays had surely been performed in this theatre.

The next day, the women stayed out of the sun, but a few of the male dancers decided to take a look at the beach. In the short time they were out in the sun, one turned the color of a ripe tomato, and another stepped on a spiny sea urchin and had to have the spines pulled out of his feet.

That evening, we put on our make-up at the hotel because the sole dressing room for the dancers, men and women, was a tent with three folding chairs, two tables, and two mirrors.

We arrived at the theatre just before the advertised start time of 9:00 PM and saw that eight thousand people had squeezed into the amphitheatre and that some of the men were carrying automatic weapons. Men covered the stage and the wings. Others perched in trees. In the distance, we could see stretchers carrying people who had been pushed off the hilly terrain and were injured. Carrying our costumes, with Algerian officials running interference, we edged our way toward the dressing room tent. In the amphitheatre, a group of young men with guns began singing a rousing song in a language I didn't recognize. Another group began singing another song and drowned out the first group. Someone told us that Ben Bella's arrival might provoke a revolution and showed us the escape route we should take if violence broke out. If given the signal, we should run as fast as we could and leave everything behind.

We waited for Ben Bella, but no one seemed to know where he was or when he would arrive. The crowd was getting rowdy. One official told us that Ben Bella had probably fled to Paris. Another told us that Ben Bella had probably fled to Egypt to hide out with President Nasser. As the noise of the impatient crowd in the amphitheatre grew louder, Madame Rosella told the Algerian officials that we needed to begin the performance immediately, but none of them were willing to start without Ben Bella. Finally, Madame Rosella took charge of the microphone, squeezed her way onto the stage, announced that we were about to begin the performance, and requested that the audience kindly clear the stage and the wings. The officials watched Madame Rosella with a combination of fear and astonishment, but people cleared the stage, and the performance began.

I performed in three ballets: *Suite Romantique*, *La Péri*, and *Pas de Quatre*. During a pose in *Suite Romantique*, I looked across the stage at my counterpart, Geneviève Masselot, a blonde who was the next shortest girl in the corps de ballet. Spectators were crammed against the stage, and an Algerian man was running his fingers up and down Geneviève's bare back.

In *La Péri*, Madame Rosella began the ballet in a tree and had to use sign language to get men out of it so that she could climb up. In *Pas de Quatre*, Maina danced her first Taglioni, and I gave my best performance of the summer. We were surrounded by mountains in a two-thousand-year-old theatre, dancing a ballet over a hundred years old for an audience of thousands of people who had probably never seen a classical ballet, and they seemed to love it. After the performance, thousands of people crowded around our tent, and the Algerian officials had to run interference again for us to get to our cars.

When we were back in Cannes, Madame Rosella told me that the Hommage au Marquis de Cuevas would be performing in Naples on October 3rd and 4th, and she wanted me to dance the solo in *La Sylphide*. She called Monsieur Lalande, the director of the theatre in Bordeaux, and got permission for me to arrive there on October 6th.

Dad didn't send a check at the end of September, and my earnings in Naples wouldn't cover the airfare to Bordeaux nor my expenses until my first paycheck on October 15th, so I walked to the post office, called Mom, and asked her to buy me an airplane ticket from Rome to Bordeaux and to send a check to the theatre in Naples. Before I left Cannes, I arranged with the Centre de Danse to pay my final bill the following month so that if I didn't get a check from Mom in Naples, which I didn't, I would have enough money for the train ticket to Rome and for two weeks of food. I hoped that I would never again be dependent on anyone else.

Naples is known for Neapolitan songs and Neapolitan ice cream and is often identified as the birthplace of pizza. The Neapolitans were more open with strangers than the French. The French didn't habitually smile at people they didn't know and were wary of people who giggled as part of their speech pattern, but Italian men seemed to need no introduction. When we walked from our hotel to the theatre, packs of young men followed us calling out, "*Bella. Bellissima.*" They seemed particularly enchanted by Geneviève with her long blond hair. In most cities we were greeted by journalists and photographers who focused on the stars. It was odd, but refreshing, to see a crowd pursuing members of the corps and ignoring the stars.

We performed at the Teatro di San Carlo, which was shaped like a horseshoe, decorated in red and gold, and had almost fifteen hundred seats. Its long history included the premieres of operas by Rossini, Donizetti, Bellini, and Verdi. The Neapolitan audiences were very enthusiastic, and I was glad Madame Rosella had given me a coda to my dance with the Hommage au Marquis de Cuevas.

I loved the Italian cuisine, especially gelato, which came in delightful flavors like hazelnut and pear as well as a deep, rich chocolate. After the second performance, I had my first fettuccini alfredo, and Madame Rosella introduced me to potato gnocchi while she talked about her day at the Roman ruins in Pompeii. That dinner was my farewell to Madame Rosella, Maina, and the other friends I wouldn't see again until the next summer.

The following morning, I woke early and took the train to Rome. Unlike Paris, which has wide vistas leading to major attractions, Rome is a city of serendipity in which treasures like the Trevi Fountain are almost hidden in a maze of streets. I marveled at the size of the Colosseum, which once seated fifty-five thousand people, and I walked up and down the broad Spanish Steps. In the preceding year, I had traveled to some interesting cities: Monte

Carlo, St-Paul-de-Vence, Paris, Bordeaux, Vichy, Deauville, Besançon, Algiers, Tipaza, Naples, and Rome. Now, I was on my way to Bordeaux for seven and a half months.

Bordeaux was less than four hundred miles from Cannes, but the Bordeaux Opera Ballet was a different world from the Hommage au Marquis de Cuevas. The Bordeaux Opera Ballet was a French company, not an international company, and the director of the theatre could hire foreign dancers only if no French dancers of equal ability could be found. For the 1963–64 season, there were four foreign dancers. Maria Santestevan, an Argentine who had danced principal roles with the de Cuevas Ballet, was the female *première étoile*. Carlos Carvajal, an American who had danced with the San Francisco Ballet and the de Cuevas Ballet, was the male *deuxième étoile* and the assistant ballet master. Jens Graff, a Norwegian who later became ballet master of the Royal Danish Ballet and director of the Norwegian National Ballet, was the *premier danseur*, and I was the *première danseuse*.

Maria Santestevan, the *première étoile*, was a petite brunette with a clean, elegant technique—more Margot Fonteyn than Rosella Hightower. She was a sweet, innocent Swanhilda, but also had the depth and maturity for Giselle. Maria had her own dressing room as did the male *première étoile*, André Médiavilla, a charming French dancer who called me Lee-Lee, a nickname that didn't catch on with anyone else.

I shared a dressing room with the two girls directly above me and below me in the hierarchy: Janine Guiton, the *deuxième étoile*, and Jacqueline Portas, the *soliste*. Janine was a curvaceous blonde with a fiery stage presence, and Jacqueline was a brunette with a beautiful line. Both girls had an impeccable sense of style and were consummate professionals.

Every spring, all of the girls below the *soliste* (the *grands sujets, petits sujets, coryphées,* and *quadrilles*) were required to attend the annual audition if they wished to be considered for the following season. Only the girls in the four top positions were exempt. The audition was held on stage, and judges were brought in from Paris. For the 1963–64 season, the auditions had been held the previous spring, but in the spring of 1964, I sneaked into the balcony and watched the female audition for the following season. Of the thirty-two girls who were chosen for positions below the *soliste*, the biggest jump up for a current dancer was eleven places, and the biggest drop down was twenty-three places. Several of the dancers for the next season were new to the company, but at the end of the audition, every girl knew exactly where she fit in the hierarchy.

When I arrived in Bordeaux, I took a taxi to the housing Carlos had found for me: a room in the home of woman whose daughter had grown up and moved out. The room had a private entrance, a comfortable bed, and a sink with running cold water. I could get hot water by lighting a burner and waiting for the water to heat up, but I usually washed my face and hands in cold water and took hot showers at the theatre.

Across the hall from my bedroom was a closet-sized room with a toilet, which was a wooden bench, enclosed in the front, with a cut-out circle in the top. Below the bench was a very long drop. The landlady kept this room spotlessly clean and odor-free. She also cleaned my bedroom and laundered the sheets and towels. Several times during the year she left me a bowl of homemade vegetable soup which I heated on the burner. The service was similar to a hotel, but I missed having social interactions with a staff and other guests. In my home, I was always alone.

The room was just over a mile from the theatre, so every morning and every night, I walked along the tree-lined Allées de Tourny, which led to the Place de la Comédie and the Bordeaux Opera House. Some mornings, when I arrived at the theatre, I saw the little girls from the Bordeaux Opera Ballet School who were called *petits rats* (little rats) because they scurried around the theatre. When I walked past the children, they curtsied and said, "Bonjour, mam'selle." All of the children knew the principal dancers by sight because our poster-size photographs hung in the lobby of the theatre.

When I entered the stage door on my first morning, the stage manager introduced herself and led me upstairs to my dressing room. It was obvious which dressing table was mine because the other two girls had already moved in. To the left of the door was a large dressing table for Janine. Along the left wall was a bed where we could nap between rehearsals and performances, and along the right wall were the dressing tables for Jacqueline and me, with Jacqueline's the one closer to the door.

I changed into a leotard and tights, pulled my hair into a ponytail, tied a chiffon scarf around it in a bow, and had just secured my hair into a bun when the stage manager informed me that the director of the theatre wanted to meet me. I looked down at my ballet slippers. "Come as you are," said the stage manager as she led the way to the office of Monsieur Lalande.

When I entered his office, the white-haired, balding Monsieur Lalande looked up from his desk and said, "My God, they've sent me a baby! What were they thinking?!" His face scowled, but his eyes twinkled. I liked him immediately. We chatted for a few minutes about Madame Rosella, and he told me that my first performance would be a pas de deux with Jens in the operetta *Les Cloches de Corneville* later that month. Monsieur Lalande would be watching the performance, as would his wife, a former dancer who was very knowledgeable and whose opinion was very important.

Monsieur Lalande had the right to fire me after my first performance, but I was confident he wouldn't. Joop van Alen (the ballet master), Carlos, and Jens had all seen me dance, and I was sure that Madame Rosella would not have put me in a position I couldn't handle.

The workday began with company class, which was actually two sequential classes: one for the principal dancers, and the other for the corps de ballet. The rehearsal room seemed small when the entire company was working together, but the result of this division was that members of the corps couldn't watch the principal dancers in class, and the principal dancers couldn't watch the corps or dancers of their own gender. In my class, when the ballet master divided us into two groups, the four girls were in one group, and the men were in the other.

In the past, I had been inspired and encouraged by other dancers. Friendly competition made us all work harder, and I was frustrated by the rigidity of the system in Bordeaux. Although the operas and operettas often used only a portion of the company, the dancers who had the night off were not allowed to buy tickets to support their colleagues, provide feedback, or see the performance from the perspective of the audience, a perspective that rejuvenates performers and allows them to experience the magic of theatre. Although I memorized the names of all of the girls in the corps de ballet, it took me weeks to put names with faces because I saw the girls in the corps only in passing.

During my rehearsals for the pas de deux in *Les Cloches de Corneville*, there were five people in the room: Joop van Alen, Carlos, Jens, the pianist, and me. The Bordeaux Opera Ballet, like the Hommage au Marquis de Cuevas, had no understudies, a policy which was never a problem in either company. As Madame Rosella said, "A dancer who doesn't dance is a dead dancer."

In Bordeaux, dancers who had not been called to a rehearsal were not allowed to watch. During this year, Maria and André did several of the famous pas de deux, including *Sleeping Beauty* and *Don Quixote*, and I would have loved to learn them, but there was no way I could sneak unnoticed into the rehearsal room, and during performances, I was often changing costumes when I wasn't on stage. At the time, I thought it was very short-sighted not to allow younger dancers to watch and learn from the dancers ranked above them, but today I can understand some of the reasons to restrict access to rehearsals. Closed rehearsals give the working dancers and choreographers the freedom to try new things and make mistakes in private. Also, dancers who watch rehearsals are giving the company free time, which puts pressure on other dancers to do the same. That pressure could cause friction not only among dancers, but also between dancers and management because the continuum of allowed-encouraged-pressured-required is a slippery slope. However, given a choice between a policy that makes people comfortable and a policy that fosters creativity and develops young dancers, I come down firmly in the camp of creativity.

In Bordeaux, I missed having Maina, José, Monsieur Robier, and Madame Rosella to give me notes and spur me on. I missed the *cantine* where the dancers socialized and exchanged ideas. I missed seeing the wide range of dancers I had seen in Madame Pereyaslavec's class and at the Centre de Danse. I missed the fresh point of view of the guest teachers Madame Rosella brought to the Centre—teachers like Edward Caton and Yves Brieux. In Bordeaux, Carlos taught morning class for the corps de ballet, and Joop van Alen taught morning class for the principals. Even with two men teaching class every morning, the dancers always had the same teacher. I missed the late-night car trips that brought dancers closer together. My everyday French was pretty good, and, in Bordeaux, strangers sometimes identified me as Niçoise, but I didn't have the vocabulary or the cultural background for complex conversations about French politics, education, contemporary literature, or a host of other subjects. In retrospect, I realize that part of my deficiency was cultural, but part was due to the fact that I was only seventeen. Carlos and Jens were both fluent in English, but I didn't see them outside of the theatre except on Christmas Day when they invited me to dinner so I wouldn't be alone. As far as I could see, in the Bordeaux Opera Ballet, people came to work, did their jobs, and went home.

I had many hours of free time. I couldn't sneak into the dance rehearsals, but I could sneak into the more-crowded singers' rehearsals, where the rehearsal-room door was often left open. I became friends with Pierrette Delange, one of the lead singers, who had a beautiful soprano voice, was an excellent actress, and had great stage presence. Pierrette was married to a baritone, and they had a little girl who was just beginning to walk. Although I was dancing in my first full-time ballet company, I spent my free time with singers.

Shortly after my debut in *Les Cloches de Corneville*, I sneaked into the wings to watch an opera. I felt a presence near my left shoulder, turned my head, and saw a frowning Monsieur Lalande.

"What are you doing here?" he whispered.

"I'm watching the opera. Isn't it wonderful?" I whispered back.

"You like opera?" he asked.

"I love it."

He frowned. "You do know you're not supposed to be here?"

"Yes," I said. "It's most unfortunate."

Monsieur Lalande beckoned for me to come into the hall where he told me that he and Madame Lalande had enjoyed my performance in *Les Cloches de Corneville*, and that his wife had informed him that I had a very strong technique as well as *fougue* (fire). He wanted me to join him and his wife in their box for the rest of the performance.

From that day forward, whenever I wasn't performing, I was watching operas and operettas from the wings. The chorus and the French singers always sang in French, but foreign artists usually sang in the languages in which the works had been written. For *La Traviata*, the chorus from Bordeaux and the tenor from the Paris Opera sang in French, but the two other guest artists, an American soprano and an Italian baritone, sang in Italian. The only production in which the chorus did not sing in French was a production of *Fidelio* for which an entire German company, including the chorus, had traveled to Bordeaux.

In addition to the operas, operettas, and ballet evenings, there were touring productions of plays, such as *The Miser* and *Of Mice and Men*. I spent almost every night in the theatre watching from the wings.

Of all of the operas, operettas, and ballet performances in which I participated, three nights were particularly memorable. The first was in November. I was in the wings warming up for the first performance of *Carmen* when Carlos arrived at the theatre and asked if I had heard the news. President Kennedy had been shot, and his condition was critical. I was stunned. I still had no access to radio or television. As I put on my make-up, I asked Janine if she thought there might be a special edition of the newspaper later in the evening. "Of course not," she said. "This isn't America." However, when I left the theatre that night, crying people filled the streets, and there was a special edition of the newspaper with the headline that Kennedy was dead.

In June of 1961, President Kennedy had charmed the French when he introduced himself as the man who accompanied Jacqueline Kennedy to Paris. Mrs. Kennedy, who spoke fluent French, was already beloved in France. She had studied at the Sorbonne, hired a French chef for the White House, wore French fashion, and was a champion of the arts. I didn't see any video of Kennedy's assassination or his funeral until I returned to the United States, but the image of people crying in the streets of Bordeaux is indelible.

The second memorable event was playing Clara in *The Nutcracker*. The choreography was a combination of the traditional Ivanov choreography and new choreography by Carlos Carvajal which put adult dancers, Jens and me, in the roles of Fritz and Clara. The story begins on Christmas Eve at a party given by the parents of Fritz and Clara. Clara and her girlfriends are playing with their dolls, rocking them to sleep, but Fritz and the other boys disrupt the girls by marching and drumming. Drosselmeyer, a mysterious magician, gives Clara a traditional nutcracker, which Fritz grabs and breaks. After the party, Clara falls asleep in the living room beside her broken nutcracker. In her dream, the Christmas tree grows to an enormous height, and Fritz's toy soldiers under the tree become life-size. Clara finds herself in a world at war: large mice, led by the multi-headed Mouse King, battle the toy soldiers, led by the Nutcracker. The Mouse King is about to kill the Nutcracker when Clara throws her slipper at the Mouse King and kills him. The Nutcracker is transformed into a prince who leads Clara through the magical Land of Snow, ruled by the Snow Queen, into the exotic Land of Sweets, ruled by the Sugar Plum Fairy. The prince tells the Sugar Plum Fairy how Clara saved his life, and in Clara's honor, the Sugar Plum Fairy dances in a celebration which includes delicacies such as chocolate from Spain, tea from China, and coffee from Arabia.

The Nutcracker is a story that resonates with girls. In the real world, grown men, like Drosselmeyer, have mysterious powers that little girls don't understand. The people charged with keeping the peace, the parents, often do nothing to curb the aggression of the boys. A girl like Clara can expect that when she grows up, the boys playing soldiers today will become real soldiers, and someone she loves may be caught in a war created by and fought by men. But in her dream, she can take action, transform the Nutcracker/soldier into a prince, and escape from a violent, male-dominated world to find peace in a society where women rule and people of all nations and ethnicities celebrate their individual cultures and join together to dance the finale in unison. The Nutcracker is an uplifting, inclusive, female empowerment story.

I loved playing Clara because of the wide range of emotions: delight with the brand-new nutcracker, irritation with Fritz as he tries to grab it, anger and hurt when the nutcracker is broken, tenderness as the nutcracker is bandaged, fear when the mice appear, triumph at killing the Mouse King, and joy and wonder in the magical new worlds. I loved hearing the audience gasp when the first mouse ran across the stage, and I loved hearing it cheer when I defeated the Mouse King. Clara was a very satisfying role.

The third memorable performance was the pas de deux *Voyage à Reims*, a technical tour de force. Carlos told me that he had choreographed this ballet for Rosella Hightower, but when he showed it to her, she laughed and said, "Find someone younger—someone who doesn't know how difficult this is." As if the combination of Rosella Hightower and difficult weren't enough catnip, Carlos, the dancer above me in the hierarchy, had chosen me to be his partner.

Most pas de deux have an adagio with the two dancers dancing together, a male variation, a female variation, and a coda that contains the most difficult steps. There are usually bows between variations, which allow the dancers to catch their breath. After the bows for the adagio, the man can breathe deeply as he walks to the starting position for his variation. After the female variation, the woman has not only her own bows, but a little time offstage as the man begins the coda. *Voyage à Reims* was solid dance with no breaks, no internal bows, and a very short solo section for Carlos. At the very end, I had a double tour en l'air. To put the difficulty in perspective, the long program in competitive figure skating is four minutes for women and four and half minutes for men, give or take ten seconds. *Voyage à Reims* was roughly double that length. In skating, the most difficult jumps are usually near the beginning when the skater is fresh. In competition, skaters get a 10 percent bonus for jumps in the second half. But dancers routinely perform the most difficult steps at the end of the program. (The Black Swan's fouettés are in the coda.) To build up stamina, I went into the studio at night and rehearsed the ballet start to finish by myself over and over and over. In performance, the atmosphere was electric. Carlos excelled as a partner, and I felt as if I had wings. During the curtain call, I was given a large bouquet of roses.

Monsieur Lalande offered me a huge raise for the following year, but I decided to leave Bordeaux. I was never comfortable in the raked studio and was concerned that if I danced exclusively on a rake for another year, my technique, especially my spins, would suffer. The divided company class, the closed rehearsal policy, and the prohibition against watching performances from the audience limited my interactions with the other dancers and with members of the audience, and I missed this communication, which promotes creativity and develops the bonds of community. During the season, no other ballet companies came to the opera house to inspire me and challenge me technically and artistically. In Bordeaux, I wasn't dancing every night like dancers in full-time ballet companies in the United States, and I didn't want to fall behind American dancers who were learning more ballets and getting more stage time. And if I were going to choose a city in which to live, I wanted a city with more sunshine, less rain, and more diversity.

At the end of the season, I wrote to Mom and Dad and told them that I would spend a few days in Paris and then fly to Geneva, but when I arrived in Geneva, ten-year-old Tuck was home alone. He told me he didn't know where the rest of the family had gone or when they'd be back. I stayed in Geneva for a couple of days in the hope that Mom or Dad might return or call, but they didn't, so I said goodbye to Tuck and flew to Cannes. For the next few years, I would see my family only once a year.

The dance landscape in Europe was much the same as the preceding year. Madame Rosella was planning a tour that would include both China and Vietnam, two countries where I still could not travel. She suggested that on my family's annual vacation in the United States, I should go to New York and see what opportunities might be there. If none of the companies had an opening, I could always do a Broadway show until they did. Madame Rosella's endorsement of Broadway raised its status in my mind, and I had loved performing in *Annie Get Your Gun*, but ever since I was ten, I had trained to become a ballet dancer, and I still wanted a career in ballet. I flew back to the United States, spent family time in Florida, and then flew to New York.

When I arrived in Manhattan, the sounds and the smells and the tastes welcomed me home. It was a joy to hear English and to understand political, literary, and cultural references. I breathed in the smell of fresh donuts that emanated from the corner donut shops, and I reacquainted myself with tuna fish salad sandwiches and BLTs on toast.

However, at Ballet Theatre, the dancers I spoke with seemed tired and frustrated. During the two years I had been in Europe, the company had weathered rough seas. The New York City Ballet had positioned itself as the home team in New York, so ABT, which spent most of its time on tour, had moved to the nation's capital to try to define itself as America's national ballet company. Unfortunately, at the same time that Ballet Theatre moved to Washington, Frederic Franklin was directing a new company in Washington, D.C., which was named the National Ballet. In December of 1963, while I was dancing *The Nutcracker* in Bordeaux, the Ford Foundation gave an astonishing 7.7 million dollars to ballet. Roughly three quarters of the money went to Balanchine; smaller grants went to regional companies, including Franklin's new company, but not one cent was allotted to Ballet Theatre. The snub was jaw-dropping and contributed to the growing power of Balanchine and the instability of Ballet Theatre. Several months later, the New York City Ballet made its move to the New York State Theater, a perfect showcase for the modern, emotionally cool Balanchine ballets. The combination of the Ford Foundation grant and the move to Lincoln Center gave Balanchine a platform far superior to any other American choreographer.

But trouble was brewing at the NYCB. When I returned to New York in the summer of 1964, some of the NYCB ballerinas who took class at Ballet Theatre were openly expressing their frustration with the attention that Balanchine was lavishing on eighteen-year-old Suzanne Farrell. The following spring, Balanchine created a sensation when he choreographed a new production of *Don Quixote* and performed the title role of Don Q. with Farrell as Dulcinea. Many dancers and dance lovers interpreted the ballet as a love letter from the sixty-one-year-old choreographer to his teenage ballerina. A few months later, Balanchine as Don Q. and Farrell as Dulcinea were on the cover of *Life* magazine. Female dancers still in their prime began leaving NYCB for other companies, a diaspora which helped to spread Balanchine's ballets, technique, and aesthetic around the world.

At the same time that the NYCB was moving into the New York State Theater, Rebekah Harkness, a supporter of the Joffrey Ballet (also snubbed by the Ford Foundation), withdrew her support from Joffrey, which forced the Joffrey Ballet to disband temporarily. Harkness declared her intention to start her own company, but in the summer of 1964, that company still seemed speculative. In fact, it was another six months before Madame Rosella wrote to me that the Harkness Ballet was opening in Cannes on

February 19th and that the studio looked like a chicken roost with dancers perched everywhere.

For an eighteen-year-old dancer who needed a steady paycheck, the New York landscape looked bleak. At Ballet Theatre, one of the dancers told me that she and her roommates had given up their apartment and moved back with their parents because ABT layoffs had left them without enough money to pay the rent. The New York City Ballet was a patriarchy in turmoil. The Joffrey Ballet, which also had a modern repertoire, was in limbo, and the Harkness Ballet was an unknown quantity. I decided to investigate the Metropolitan Opera Ballet.

I walked to the grand old Metropolitan Opera House and took class with Antony Tudor in the rooftop studio. After class, Mr. Tudor told me that Dame Alicia Markova had been hired to turn the Metropolitan Opera Ballet into a world-class company that would have ballet evenings both at the Metropolitan Opera House and in other venues. This sounded like a fantastic opportunity. With Dame Alicia at the helm, I knew the company would be dancing the classics. Mr. Tudor introduced me to Dame Alicia, a petite, dark-haired woman in her fifties, who was always dressed and coiffed as if she were ready for a photo shoot. Dame Alicia told me she had no openings in the company at the present time; however, if I could stay in New York and dance in the opera *Samson and Delilah*, which had scattered performances throughout the season, she could take me into the company full-time in March when one of the girls was leaving to get married. The Met contract would be fifty-two weeks a year with paid vacation and pension and health benefits. Because of the sporadic rehearsal and performance schedule for *Samson and Delilah*, I couldn't dance with another company or perform in a Broadway show to pay the rent. I had banked one-third of my gross salary in Bordeaux, but in New York, that would last only until November. I wrote to Mom and Dad, and Dad agreed to support me for a few months to get me through the winter.

In August, 1964, I went to the business office of the Metropolitan Opera Company to sign my contract for the 1965 spring tour, a contract which included an option for my services for the 1965–66 season. As a condition of employment, I had to join a union, the American Guild of Musical Artists (AGMA). My contract indicated that the rules of AGMA were incorporated into the contract, so I asked to see the rules. The man in the office laughed. The rules were a thick book, he told me. No one ever asked to see them. I insisted that I had to know what I was signing, so he sent for the book, and I sat in the office and read it.

As long as I was an extra dancer, I would be paid a performance rate and an hourly rate for rehearsals. Once I was under contract, I would have a weekly salary plus pension and health benefits. There was a box on the health form that had to be checked if I wanted pregnancy benefits. I asked if the pregnancy benefits were an additional charge and was told they were not, so I checked the box, signed the contract, and was committed to the Metropolitan Opera Ballet for the next two years—assuming the company picked up its option.

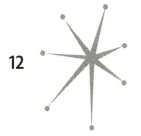

12 Alicia Markova and the
Metropolitan Opera Ballet,
1964–1967

The two constants in my life were Madame Per-
eyaslavec's class at the Ballet Theatre School on Fifty-Seventh Street, and
rehearsals and performances at the Metropolitan Opera House on Thirty-
Ninth Street. Perfectly situated between the two was the Washington Jefferson Hotel, a comfortable hotel on Fifty-First Street just off Eighth Avenue. This neighborhood was called Hell's Kitchen and was considered
to be dicey, but the streets were always filled with people, and I never felt
that I was in danger. The hotel was half a block from the Eighth Avenue
Howard Johnson's Motor Lodge and across the street from Tout Va Bien, a
family-owned French restaurant. The Washington Jefferson had a twenty-
four-hour doorman to ensure that I got home safely, a twenty-four-hour
desk clerk to take messages (essential for a dancer who didn't report to the
theatre every day), and a pay phone in the lobby. My room was small, but

it had running hot and cold water, daily maid service, free stationery, and communal bathrooms down the hall. The hotel cost 15 percent less than my parents had paid the minister and his wife two years earlier and was much more conveniently located.

I loved being back in midtown Manhattan, surrounded by theatres and restaurants. In September, the Kirov Ballet came to the Met, and I saw Alla Sizova in *Cinderella* and Natalia Makarova in *Swan Lake*. Both performances were fantastic. On Broadway, *Fiddler on the Roof*, directed and choreographed by Jerome Robbins, was opening at the Imperial Theatre. The cast included Sharon Lerit, the dancer from the Ballet Theatre School who had played the Sad Girl in *Bye, Bye, Birdie*. Richard Burton was playing the lead role in *Hamlet* with an all-star cast. This play was so popular that two performances were beamed live into movie theatres by Electronovision, and I was able to see one of them. Madame Pereyaslavec's morning class still showcased an ever-changing array of talent. New York was providing the inspiration I had missed in Bordeaux.

The third constant in my life was Columbia University. My tenth grade biology teacher from Tatnall, Dr. Lincoln Hanson, was now teaching psychology at Columbia and invited me to sit in on his classes. I decided to register at Columbia and take two courses: psychology and German.

Zachary Solov choreographed the ballet in *Samson and Delilah*, and we rehearsed in the rooftop studio overlooking the city. Although I was just an extra dancer, everyone in the company was very friendly, and Audrey Keane, the ballet mistress, was a perfect den mother. I loved performing in the historic theatre that had captured my imagination during my first trip to New York, and I liked being back in a dressing room packed with other girls. Sometimes, between rehearsals, some of the girls would eat at a luncheonette which had barrels of pickles on the tables. I always ordered vanilla ice cream because it was a perfect food: it didn't weigh me down; the cream had staying power, and the sugar gave me quick energy. However, I knew that a balanced diet required vegetables, so I ate pickles while I waited for my ice cream. One day, one of the girls told me that the front office was very curious about this new girl who looked like a baby, ate pickles and ice cream, and wanted pregnancy benefits. I assured her that I had requested pregnancy benefits because I expected that at some future date I might get married (which I did five years later) and that I wanted to make sure I would have pregnancy benefits at that time. Management need not worry about my getting pregnant in the near future. Like many dancers my age, I still had no dating experience except for high school dances.

My biggest concern that fall was that I didn't see Dame Alicia. I heard that she had fallen and injured her leg, but it seemed to me that fall or no fall, the director of a company should be at the theatre on a daily basis, and it bothered me that the company rarely saw her.

I needed new leotards, but my budget was tight, so I went to Woolworth's basement and bought a three-pack of little boys' white t-shirts to wear with black trunks. This gave me three close-fitting tops for less than the cost of one leotard. White was an accepted color in Madame Pereyaslavec's class, but I had never seen girls in t-shirts, so I was a bit nervous the first morning I wore one to the morning class. Madame Pereyaslavec made her grand entrance, surveyed the room, and began the pliés. During the exercise, she came over to me and said very quietly, "Is all right. When you get in company, you buy leotards."

Throughout the winter, I took Madame Pereyaslavec's morning class at Ballet Theatre and occasional evening classes at Ballet Arts with some of the Metropolitan Opera dancers. As spring approached, I realized that I needed a back-up job after the tour in case the Met didn't exercise its option, so I decided to audition for a revival of *Carousel* at the New York State Theater. The show would star John Raitt, the star of the original Broadway production, and would feature the original choreography of Agnes de Mille re-created by Gemze de Lappe.

When I arrived at the artists' entrance, the building seemed cold and corporate—almost like a prison compared to the grand old Metropolitan Opera House and the historic theatres in Europe. Inside the artists' entrance, at a fortress-like desk, were two guards in uniform. I explained that I wanted to attend the dance audition for *Carousel*, and one of the guards told me to sign in and take the self-service elevator upstairs. When I exited the elevator, I saw a middle-aged man sitting on a chair across from the elevator. I peered down a corridor. "May I help you?" the man asked. I explained that I was looking for the ladies' dressing room, and the man said he would escort me to the door, which he did.

After changing into my pink tights, white t-shirt, and black trunks, I went into the audition room where I heard girls whispering that Richard Rodgers was there. "Where?" I asked. They pointed at the nice man who had escorted me down the hall.

The Agnes de Mille choreography was right up my alley, and I was one of the dancers chosen for the show. I explained my situation with the Metropolitan Opera and was told that *Carousel* would hold the job open until they heard from me in May.

During the winter, I hadn't seen any evidence that Dame Alicia was renovating the company, but in the spring of 1965, there were several encouraging signs. First, the April 10th edition of *Opera News* had a five-page article about the Metropolitan Opera Ballet, and I learned that Ivan Allen, a soloist at the Met, had been a principal at Ballet Theatre, and that there were quite a few other dancers who had danced at Ballet Theatre, Ballet Russe, the National Ballet of Canada, and Ballet Rambert. Second, on April 11th, the ballet gave a performance at the Met that was very good and very well received. Finally, Anna Aragno, a lovely Italian dancer I knew from Madame Pereyaslavec's class, was also planning to join the company. Anna and I were the same size, but had contrasting personalities. In *Pas de Quatre* I would have cast her as Grisi: clean, precise, and perfect. She would be a terrific addition to the company.

The Metropolitan Opera spring tour was a high point of the year. After seven months in Manhattan, the company embarked on a six-week tour to Boston, Cleveland, Atlanta, Memphis, Dallas, St. Louis, Minneapolis, and Detroit. There were few rehearsals on tour, and, for the ballet, only a few performances a week. We had plenty of time for parties, sightseeing, and enjoying our hotels with swimming pools.

I was performing in three operas: *Samson and Delilah*, *Aida*, and *The Last Savage*. Katherine Dunham, an African-American choreographer and anthropologist, had choreographed *Aida*. In New York, the dark-skinned

Nubians were danced by members of the Katherine Dunham company, but for budgetary reasons, when the Metropolitan Opera went on tour, dancers in the full-time company took over these roles. (On a later tour, we also replaced children in the children's chorus in *La Bohème*.) In 1965, the only African-American dancer in our company was male, and I was cast as a Nubian. I wore a chocolate brown unitard and painted my face and hands chocolate brown. The choreography was unlike any I had ever done: in one step, I leaned forward from the hips so that my upper body was parallel with the floor. My arms swung like propellers and banged on my butt. The high-energy choreography was exhilarating, and after the performance, the dark body paint came off my skin much more easily than the blue body paint I would wear during the next season when I was a Bedouin. In *The Last Savage*, I played a servant boy, a comedic, non-dancing role. This was my favorite role of the three because I loved hearing the audience laugh. The spring tours were a marvelous opportunity to stretch our techniques and play roles we couldn't play in New York.

In the mid-1960s, the company traveled by train. Train A was for the orchestra and the ballet. Train B was for the singers, management, and the technical staff. Train B always left at least half an hour before Train A so that the technical staff would arrive first. The dancers were placed two to a sleeper compartment, and on my first tour, I shared a compartment with Miyoko Kato, another dancer who was engaged for the tour with an option for the following season.

All of the dancers were required to be well dressed getting on and off the train, but once we were on the train, many of the girls changed into caftans or slacks, and the parties began. In Boston, some of us took class with Virginia Williams, an excellent teacher who was founder and artistic director of the Boston Ballet, and whose studio had a pole in the middle. In Cleveland, we also took class at a local studio, and the opening night party was one of the biggest and most elegant on the tour. In Atlanta, I sat by the pool at the Peachtree Inn, and many of the musicians' and singers' wives flew in for the week, but there was no big opening night party. One of the dancers told me that in the past, the Atlanta party had been one of the best, but when superstar soprano Leontyne Price came on tour, the hostess of the party told Rudolf Bing, the general manager of the Met, to make sure that Leontyne Price understood that she wasn't invited because they didn't allow Negros as guests at their parties. Mr. Bing informed the hostess that if Leontyne Price weren't invited, he would direct the company to boycott the party. The hostess cancelled the party, and during the three years I was on tour with the ballet, there was never a big opening night party in Atlanta.

In the 1950s and 1960s, the arts were more inclusive than mainstream society. In 1954, the Supreme Court ruled in *Brown v. Board of Education* that the "separate, but equal" doctrine of racial segregation in schools was unconstitutional. Nevertheless, three years later, Governor Orval Faubus of Arkansas mobilized the Arkansas National Guard to prevent nine black students from entering a white high school in Little Rock, and President Eisenhower had to send the U.S. Army to escort the children inside. In downtown Wilmington during the 1950s, St. Andrew's Church was the white Episcopal Church, and St. Matthew's was the black Episcopal Church. When I was dancing in *A Chorus Line* in Los Angeles, Sammy Davis, Jr., a movie star, stage star, and member of the "Rat Pack," told me that during the 1950s, he couldn't stay in the Las Vegas hotels in which he performed because Negros weren't allowed to stay in the guest rooms. Interracial marriage was illegal in some states until 1967 when the Supreme Court, in a unanimous decision, struck down Virginia's anti-miscegenation law, "The Racial Integrity Act of 1924."

At the end of the 1950s, there were many famous black dancers, including Josephine Baker, the Nicholas Brothers, and Charles "Honi" Coles. There were also dance companies that showcased black dancers, such as the interracial Alvin Ailey American Dance Theater and the Katherine Dunham Dance Company. In the 1960s, Alvin Ailey and Katherine Dunham also choreographed for the Metropolitan Opera and on Broadway. At the New York City Ballet, Arthur Mitchell became a star in 1957 when George Balanchine choreographed *Agon*, a sensual pas de deux for Mitchell and Diana Adams. A black man handling a white woman clad only in leotards and tights was pushing the envelope at a time when white married couples on television slept in twin beds. In 1969, Mitchell co-founded a classical ballet company for black dancers, Dance Theatre of Harlem.

At the Metropolitan Opera, during the mid-1960s, there were African-Americans in the ballet, the chorus, and among the lead singers. Star soprano Martina Arroyo, of African-American and Puerto Rican descent, gave wonderful spaghetti parties to which she invited stars and dancers, management and secretaries. We were young and not so young; black, brown, and white; male and female; rich and just getting by. Martina made all of us welcome and all of us laugh.

In 1973, I was on tour again—this time with my then-husband, Raymond Gibbs, a tenor who was singing the role of Macduff in *Macbeth* and standing by for Franco Corelli as Romeo. We attended a dinner party in Atlanta that introduced Schuyler Chapin, the new general manager of the Metropolitan Opera, to the Atlanta opera supporters. The woman seated beside me told me how happy they were to welcome Schuyler Chapin because they didn't like Rudolf Bing, who was arrogant and unbearably rude. "How dare he tell us who we can invite to our parties," she said, as others nodded in agreement.

If this was high society, I wanted no part of it.

After Atlanta, the company spent a few days in Memphis. I visited the lovely Peabody Hotel, where a brace of ducks lived in the penthouse. Every day, the ducks would come down the elevator and walk along a red carpet to a pond in the lobby. At the end of the day, the red carpet was rolled out again, and the ducks waddled back to the penthouse. In Dallas, St. Louis, Minneapolis, and Detroit, I spent my days by the pool and my nights at parties or at the theatre. Halfway through the tour, the Met picked up the option to my contract, and I turned down the job in *Carousel*.

When I returned to New York, I took my final examinations at Columbia. I received A's in both courses, but my German teacher informed me that the head of the German department was livid that the best exam that semester had come from a girl who had missed six weeks of classes and had demanded that the Dean of Students enforce the attendance rule beginning with the next semester. The rule stated that students were allowed only two absences; the third triggered an F. I tried to convince the Assistant Dean that if I missed a third class, I should receive an incomplete, rather than an

F, but my request was denied. The Assistant Dean told me that he couldn't bend the rules, but he could give me a scholarship if I wanted to attend Columbia full time. I declined. The university would be there in ten or twenty years. A dance career would not.

After the spring tour, the Metropolitan Opera Ballet had performances at Lewisohn Stadium in upper Manhattan and at the Long Island Festival on Long Island. I danced in two ballets: *Les Sylphides* and *Polovetsian Dances*. During rehearsals, Dame Alicia was walking with a cane, but as she staged *Les Sylphides*, the quality of her upper body movement indicated why she had become a star. Dame Alicia was in her mid-fifties, but she seemed older. Her energy level was low; her voice was a whisper, and on the rare occasions she gave company class, her pliés were like tai chi on Valium. Nevertheless, when she was staging ballets, she was engaged, demanding, and detail-oriented.

Because the Metropolitan Opera had picked up my option, I couldn't dance in *Carousel*, but I did go to see the show, and I loved Agnes de Mille's choreography, especially in "Louise's Ballet." I could see myself as Louise, a teenage girl who is an outsider in her town and longs for someone—anyone—to accept her. In the early 1970s, I finally got the opportunity to play Louise opposite the original Broadway star, John Raitt, who was still terrific in the role of Billy Bigelow and who also directed the production. The choreographer was Clint Hamblin, who did not recreate the de Mille choreography, but choreographed a beautiful, well-reviewed ballet. Clint was an outstanding partner, and the role of Louise is one of my all-time favorite roles.

The 1965–66 Metropolitan Opera season opened on September 29, 1965, with a new production of *Faust* directed by Jean-Louis Barrault and choreographed by Flemming Flindt. Like the ballet in *Samson and Delilah*, the Walpurgis Night Ballet in *Faust* was a bacchanal. During rehearsals, I enjoyed eavesdropping on Barrault and Flindt as they commented on the dancers in French.

The second night of the season, I performed in a new production of *Queen of Spades*, which was choreographed by Dame Alicia. The ballet was simple and elegant with eighteenth-century costumes, wigs, and shoes with heels.

It was still fall when ballet mistress Audrey Keane informed me that I would be dancing one of the plum roles of the season: the Circus Ballerina in *La Périchole*. This was a solo on pointe that got billing the same size as the lead singers. Anna Aragno would dance the first performances; I would dance the last. Audrey followed this excellent news by saying that it was very unusual for first-year dancers to get such a high-profile role. However, Cyril Ritchard, the director of *La Périchole*, had rejected the dancers originally cast—dancers with more seniority—and threatened to bring in two dancers from the New York City Ballet if the Met couldn't meet his standards. As soon as I found out that casting was affected by seniority, I knew that my future was not at the Met.

Every day, as I walked to the Metropolitan Opera House, I passed through the Broadway theatre district. I watched the ever-changing marquees as new stars joined hit shows and less successful shows opened and closed. I learned that on Broadway, dancers didn't sign contracts for a year; they could give two weeks' notice and move on to a new show. Dancers also knew who would be choreographing a show before they auditioned. Broadway gave dancers much more freedom than ballet companies. I learned that new musicals had out-of-town tryouts before they opened on Broadway, and that the shows went on national tours if they became hits. I saw singers and dancers choose audition songs at Colony Music, compete for jobs, and go out for coffee afterwards. On matinee days, restaurants were filled with singers and dancers having dinner together. This was the same camaraderie I had enjoyed at the Centre de Danse.

That season, *Fiddler on the Roof, Funny Girl,* and *Hello, Dolly!* were dazzling entertainment, but they also touched a deeper chord. I came out of the theatres with a better understanding of myself and the world around me because of the people and situations I had seen in these shows. I wanted to become a part of this magical, musical, mind-expanding world. I began taking voice lessons twice a week.

At the end of one of my lessons, an agent stopped by to see my teacher and told me that Kermit Bloomgarden was looking for a young girl for the lead in a new play, *The Playroom*. The agent told me he would call the producer and arrange for me to pick up the script.

The audition was held on the stage of a Broadway theatre, and after I read, the voices in the dark asked me about my acting experience. I told them about my roles in ballets and operas. They asked about my experience in straight plays, which was nil. They asked where I had studied acting, and I told them that I hadn't. The voices told me that they couldn't give the lead in a Broadway show to someone with no experience, but that I should get into an acting class because they believed I could have a future as an actress.

I researched acting teachers and enrolled at the HB Studio, which had classes on Sunday, my only day off from the Met. Broadway was looking like a viable option.

My take-home pay at the Met for a six-day week was $82.52. Waitresses at Howard Johnson's took home around $150 for five days' work, and one of the most popular waitresses told me that she usually made $250. Nevertheless, I put money in the bank every week. When the Metropolitan Opera went on tour, I checked out of the Washington Jefferson Hotel and packed everything I owned into a suitcase and a trunk. I carried the suitcase on the train, and the trunk was delivered to the theatres along with the sets and costumes. On tour, I lived on my per diem and banked my salary. I was building a war chest so that I could leave the Met.

That February, shortly after I danced the Circus Ballerina in *La Périchole*, I auditioned for a production of the musical *Where's Charley?*, which was scheduled to open at City Center the last week of May for a two-week run. When I was offered the show, I told the producer that I would have to ask Dame Alicia to release me from the last three weeks of the spring tour. I knew that Dame Alicia might take offense that I wanted to do the musical instead of finishing the tour, but I thought the opportunity was worth the risk. I hadn't seen any progress toward a world-class company at the Met, and with ABT back in New York and NYCB the resident company at the New York State Theater, a classical company at the Met seemed unlikely. *Where's Charley?* was the perfect opportunity to get a taste of Broadway and to get my Equity card, the Broadway union card, so I wrote to Dame Alicia and asked for permission to do the musical. She denied my request.

That spring, the Metropolitan Opera Ballet performed the American premiere of Antony Tudor's *Echoing of Trumpets*, the world premiere of Tudor's *Concerning Oracles*, and the American premiere of Bournonville's *La Ventana*. Antony Tudor staged both of his ballets, and Hans Brenaa staged *La Ventana*. The fact that Dame Alicia didn't stage a new ballet for any of our spring performances told me that her importance to the company was waning.

It may seem odd that I never auditioned for Ballet Theatre, but in the summer of 1964, Dame Alicia's invitation to join the Metropolitan Opera Ballet had seemed like a terrific opportunity, and I committed myself to the company for two years. By the spring of 1966, my heart belonged to Broadway.

Nevertheless, there were good reasons to stay at the Met for one more year. The 1966–67 season would be the first season in Lincoln Center. This would be an exciting, historic season, and I wanted to be a part of it. Also, although I was two for two with musical theatre auditions, I knew that my success might be beginner's luck, and if it took me a few months to get a Broadway show, I wanted more money in the bank so that I never again had to rely on my parents. Finally, the Met Opera Ballet kept me in New York where I could study voice and acting, and where the new Metropolitan Opera House had soundproof rooms with pianos where I could learn new songs and vocalize every day. I signed a contract for one more year.

On September 16, 1966, the Metropolitan Opera gave its first performance in the new house in Lincoln Center. The auditorium was red and gold with a horseshoe of Austrian crystal chandeliers that floated toward the ceiling as the house lights dimmed. A new opera, *Antony and Cleopatra* by Samuel Barber, was commissioned for the occasion, and the set was predominately gold. Franco Zeffirelli designed and staged the production, and Alvin Ailey choreographed. The opening night audience included Mrs. Lyndon Baines Johnson (the wife of the President), Nelson Rockefeller (the governor of New York), John D. Rockefeller III (philanthropist and brother of the governor), and John Lindsay (the mayor of New York).

It was a glamorous opening, but morale in the ballet was plummeting.

Millions of dollars had been spent on the overproduced *Antony and Cleopatra*, while the orchestra, which far out-earned dancers, had gone on strike for higher pay. The dancers earned in a six-day week what local bartenders earned in two nights. At the Met, the ballet was at the bottom of the totem pole in pay and respect, and that season management decided the dancers should also perform as supernumeraries. No one told us that we were to be supers when the cast list was posted for *Die Frau ohne Schatten*, but as the date of the dress rehearsal approached, we learned that there was no actual choreography; we would be posed on elevators as soon as the elevators were functioning properly. A few days before the premiere, when the elevators still weren't working, one of the dancers told Dame Alicia about an industrial show for a new car in which the elevator malfunctioned and the car crashed through the wooden floor as a mangled mass of metal. An hour later, the ballet was out of *Die Frau ohne Schatten*.

Shortly afterward, the ballet was cast in *Elektra* to perform stylized movement. When the dancers realized that the stylized movement consisted only of running around the set, they clomped so loudly that Birgit Nilsson, rumored to be the highest-paid soprano in the world, went directly to Mr. Bing's office and said, "They go, or I go." The ballet was out of *Elektra*.

Many of the dancers had husbands or boyfriends in New York and liked having nights off. I didn't. I wanted to be on stage every single night. But I didn't want to be scenery. I wanted to dance, and at the Met, I wasn't dancing enough. I could hardly wait to audition for Broadway shows where I would be guaranteed eight shows a week.

The greatest indignity of the season was our banishment from the red carpet. After we entered the stage door and showed our picture IDs to the guards, we walked down a red-carpeted hallway, parallel to stage left (audience right). At the end of the corridor, we turned left and continued on the red carpeting along the back wall of the stage. To our left was the stage; to our right, the star dressing rooms and the loading dock. The dancers' dressing rooms were stage right (audience left). One day, Audrey informed us that we were no longer allowed to walk across the back of the stage, but would have to take the elevator down one floor, walk in the narrow walkway behind the orchestra pit on level A (a walkway which had a low beam and would require the taller dancers to duck), and then take the elevator up one level to the dressing rooms on the main floor. The rumor we heard was that management didn't want the ballet dancers to wear out the red carpet. This was absurd. Hundreds of audience members walked on the red carpet every night after the performance to meet the lead singers and get autographs. We demanded a meeting with Herman Krawitz, one of the four assistant general managers. When confronted, Mr. Krawitz assured us that the rule had nothing to do with protecting the carpet; management was concerned about our health: we might catch cold if we passed by the open loading dock in freezing weather. An indignant dancer spoke up: "Mr. Krawitz, when we walk by the loading dock, we are coming from or going to the stage door. In freezing weather, we're wearing our coats, hats, gloves, and scarves. If we don't catch cold on Sixty-Fifth Street, we won't catch cold passing the loading dock." We never did find out why management wanted us to detour, but by speaking up, we earned the right to take a direct route to our dressing rooms.

These problems were solved in a reasonably private manner, but the "Dance of the Hours" in *La Gioconda* was a public embarrassment. We had several weeks of rehearsal for this important pointe ballet. However, choreographer Zachary Solov evidently failed to consult with the set and costume designers. At our first stage rehearsal, Solov had to re-choreograph the ballet to accommodate the set. At the dress rehearsal, as we folded our bodies into the "dying swan" pose, our headdresses, which had metal wires sticking up like a fan of crochet hooks, hooked into the mesh of our skirts, and we couldn't sit up without tearing the skirts. The orchestra sputtered to a stop. Still folded in half, we rolled onto our sides so that the stagehands and the male dancers could untangle the hooks. Zachary Solov re-choreographed again, but our first performance was a shambles.

Walter Terry wrote about the "near-disaster" of *La Gioconda* and the demoralization of the ballet in an article entitled "Bad Deal for Ballet at the Met," in the *New York World Journal Tribune* of December 4, 1966. Terry wrote that the male lead in *La Gioconda* was so bad that he should have been summarily fired. Terry also wrote that some of the best dancers had left the company. In fact, all three dancers who had been billed as principals during the 1964–65 season had left the company by the spring of 1966. Our 1966 summer ballet program had listed dancers only as soloists or corps de ballet—neither an encouraging sign for the future nor good for morale. Terry's article also informed us that the ballet evening scheduled for the spring had been cancelled.

Nevertheless, the Metropolitan Opera Ballet was a terrific job for dancers who needed a steady paycheck, wanted to spend most of the year in New York, liked to perform a wide range of dance styles, or loved opera. The spring tours were practically paid vacations, and in the summer, we had several weeks off with pay. We worked with great choreographers and directors. We could watch performances from B box, the company box, which, to my astonishment, was rarely full. We had access to soundproof studios with pianos. We had understudies, so that dancers who were sick had the option of staying home. Two of the assistant general managers, John Gutman and Francis Robinson, were particularly supportive of the dancers, and both helped me in my goal of dancing on Broadway. Mr. Gutman, who ran the Met Studio for young singers, gave me a ten-lesson scholarship for voice lessons, and Mr. Robinson suggested that I might act in television commercials and gave me a letter of introduction to an agent at the Ashley-Famous Agency, part of today's ICM Partners. As disappointed as I was that the Metropolitan Opera Ballet didn't realize its potential, I owed a lot to the Met, including financial stability.

By spring, I was eager to audition for Broadway. Madame Rosella and Maina had kept me apprised of the dance scene in Europe, and Madame Rosella wrote that she could always find me a place in a European company, but she agreed that it might be time to try Broadway. "Why not?" she wrote. I informed the Met that I was not going to renew my contract after it expired on June 25th, and I set my sights on the Great White Way.

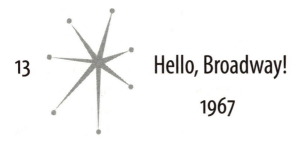

13 Hello, Broadway!
1967

My first audition that spring was for *Henry, Sweet Henry*, a new musical based on the film *The World of Henry Orient*. I went to the open call (open to all dancers, union and non-union) because I wasn't yet a member of Actors' Equity, the Broadway union. After each dance combination, some of the girls were eliminated. Finally, the few remaining girls were asked to sing. I sang a sweet soprano song, and Michael Bennett, the choreographer, asked me if I had a belt song. I had no idea what he meant. Michael hopped up on stage, took me by the hand, led me to the piano, and played a note. "Yell that note," he said. So I did. He played a few more notes, and I yelled them. "Good," he said. "Here's what I want you to do. Go to Colony Music and buy the song 'Consider Yourself' from *Oliver!* Then come yell it for me at the callback." This was great. Not only did I have the callback, but my song would be exactly what Michael Bennett wanted to hear.

At the callback, union and non-union girls all danced together. As before, I made it through all of the dancing and was asked to sing. I now knew that a belt song is a song that can be sung loudly in the lower register of a woman's voice. I sang "Consider Yourself" and sang it pretty well. Some of the other girls had better voices and more polished vocal performances, but none were better dancers. Finally, after the last girl sang, Michael Bennett called out the names of the girls he wanted to hire, one after another. He didn't call my name. All of the girls who got into the show were hugging each other, and I wanted to sink into the floor.

This was my first experience with public rejection. In my five years as a professional ballet dancer, I had never done a formal audition, much less been rejected. I wondered what I had done wrong.

Nine years later, when I was performing in *A Chorus Line* in Los Angeles, I learned why I hadn't been hired. I was having lunch with Baayork Lee, the dance captain for *A Chorus Line*, who had been in the original cast of *Henry, Sweet Henry*. Baayork mentioned that when I came on stage to audition for *A Chorus Line*, Bob Avian, the co-choreographer with Michael Bennett, leaned over to her and whispered, "That's the girl from the *Henry, Sweet Henry* audition." I asked Baayork why I hadn't been hired for that show, and she said that by the time I auditioned, Michael had already promised more jobs than he had.

By 1976, I understood that companies sometimes held auditions when there were no jobs available, that is, when the union requires auditions or when the company is looking for future replacements, but in 1967, when I was new at auditioning, I was sure I had done something wrong.

Fortunately, on Broadway, there are always more shows and more auditions. I auditioned for *Robert and Elizabeth*, a musical based on the love story of Robert Browning and Elizabeth Barrett Browning. This show was already a hit in London, so it had a better than average chance of succeeding on Broadway. I had high hopes of getting the show because the choreographer, Matt Mattox, was known for challenging choreography, and the more challenging the choreography, the less competition I would have. Also, it was a period piece, which meant that the dances would probably be based on classic dance forms like ballet rather than on contemporary dances like the twist, the swim, or the funky chicken, which were more challenging for me than fouettés, splits, and five pirouettes.

I went to the open call and made the callbacks. At the final audition, we danced for hours as Matt Mattox eliminated one dancer after another. He asked for fouettés, which only I could do well. He asked for difficult acrobatics, which only one other girl could do. Then we sang. Finally, he chose four girls, and I was one of the four. I had my first Broadway show! "Congratulations," he said. "Make sure we have your mailing address. You will receive your contracts in a couple of weeks."

I was walking on air for the next few weeks. I thought it would be pointless and dishonest to audition for other shows when I already had a job, so I took class with Madame Pereyaslavec and waited for my contract. And waited. And waited. Finally, I received a letter from the producers explaining that due to legal problems, they could not present the show at that time. I had burned through weeks of savings and was back to square one.

In the trade papers *Show Business* and *Backstage*, I read of an upcoming audition for the Vietnam tour of *Hello, Dolly!* I had no interest in going to a war zone halfway around the world, but I had been advised by a Broadway veteran to audition for *everything* until I was known, so I went to the audition. Once again, I attended the open call, which was immediately after the Equity call. Joe Helms, the dance captain of the Broadway company, gave the audition. I enjoyed performing the breezy choreography of Gower Champion. The dances were filled with joy, and compared to the Matt Mattox audition, a piece of cake. Only a few girls were asked to sing, and after we had sung, Joe thanked us for coming.

As I picked up my dance bag, Joe walked over to me and asked, "Why don't I know you?" I told him that I had been dancing in ballet companies. "I really like the way you dance," he said. "I'll tell you the situation. For the Vietnam tour, we gave priority to girls who had already done the show on Broadway. I only needed a couple more girls, and I found them this morning at the Equity call. Would you be at all interested in the Broadway company?"

I was definitely interested.

"Good," he said. "One of the twins is leaving for another show, and we need to replace her. Are you willing to dye your hair blonde?"

"Absolutely," I said.

"Good," he said. "You'll hear from us in a day or two."

And I did. The next week was a whirlwind of activity. I joined Actors' Equity Association and signed my first Equity contract. I went to an elegant salon, chosen and paid for by the producer, where my hair was dyed golden blonde. I rehearsed with Joe in a studio during the day and watched the show at the St. James Theatre at night. It was strange to rehearse without the other dancers. I had to imagine the people who would surround me, and I had to imagine the sets. The girl playing my twin, Linda Bonem, was a girl I knew from ballet class, and she seemed absolutely delighted that I was joining the cast and introduced me to all the other girls.

My first performance was a Wednesday matinee, and my put-in rehearsal with the other dancers was that same day at noon. I arrived an hour early, changed into my leotard, and warmed up. At two minutes to noon, the other dancers drifted in, holding paper cups of coffee and chomping on bagels. They marked the choreography, rather than dancing full-out, but at least I got a sense of who was around me and how much space I had.

After the rehearsal, I put on my make-up, pulled my blonde hair into pig-tails, and walked down to the basement where a dresser helped me into my blue-and-white sailor costume for the opening number. At the five-minute call, I went up onto the stage and danced a few steps in the boots that I was wearing for the first time. I examined the set pieces, both on stage and in the wings. At the final call, "places," I picked up my prop, a newspaper. As some of the other dancers took their opening positions on stage, I went into the wings and stood beside my twin, who wished me luck.

At precisely 2:08 PM, the overture for the matinee began, and the music from *Hello, Dolly!* filled the St. James Theatre. A tingle of excitement ran through my body. I took my position on a cart offstage right. Betty Grable, the movie star and #1 pin-up girl during World War II, was playing Dolly. She joined me on the cart and whispered, "What's your name?"

"Lee," I said.

"I'm Betty," she said. "Welcome to the company."

In unison, we held our newspapers in front of our faces. As the opening number began, the cart rolled onto the stage. On cue, Betty Grable lowered her newspaper, and the audience erupted into applause. The first act flew by. I bounded from one dance number to the next: "Put on Your Sunday Clothes," "Dancing," and "Before the Parade Passes By." Between numbers, I ran downstairs, changed from one beautiful dress to another, and ran back up into the wings. I reveled in the freedom of Gower Champion's choreography, and after a year in the huge, modern Metropolitan Opera House in Lincoln Center, I loved the intimacy and the elegance of the St. James Theatre. During the second act of the show, I stood in the wings and watched the chorus of singing and dancing waiters perform the jubilant title song, "Hello, Dolly!"—a song which welcomes Dolly Levi back to the Harmonia Gardens Restaurant—back to the place where she belongs. And I knew then, as surely as I knew at age eight that I was going to work, that I had found the place where I belonged.

For the next twenty-five years, I performed in musicals, plays, industrial shows, summer stock, dinner theatre, television, and film.

In November of 1967, producer David Merrick replaced our all-white cast of *Hello, Dolly!* with an all-black cast starring Pearl Bailey. Within days, I had my next Broadway show, *Here's Where I Belong*, a musical *East of Eden*, which ran only one night on Broadway, but allowed me to work with choreographers Hanya Holm and Tony Mordente. I segued into *Oklahoma!* at the Paper Mill Playhouse where Gemze de Lappe recreated the original Agnes de Mille choreography. The show was a joy, and when it ended, I was offered a job as a replacement in another David Merrick show, *How Now Dow Jones*, no audition required. In one year, I had added *Oklahoma!* and three Broadway shows to my resume.

The shows tumbled by, one after another. In *The Love Match*, Danny Daniels choreographed two show-stopping numbers. One night, we got a standing ovation in the middle of the show, but *The Love Match* didn't make it to Broadway. I performed in *Oklahoma!* at the New York State Theater, and Gemze de Lappe introduced us to Agnes de Mille, who demonstrated some of the movements and gave us additional insight into their origins and execution. In *La Strada,* a musical based on the Fellini film, Alvin Ailey choreographed a beautiful pas de deux for me and one of the men, which the director promptly cut. Alvin was wonderful. The director was not, and by the time I gave my two weeks notice in Detroit, many cast members had preceded me out the door.

I played Liesl in *The Sound of Music* at the Jones Beach Theatre, an outdoor amphitheatre with more than eight thousand seats where we performed rain or shine and were ferried to an island stage by boat. I played Patty in the original Broadway production of *You're a Good Man, Charlie Brown* at the Golden Theatre, one of the smallest Broadway houses, but still too big for the show. In dinner theatres, I interspersed musical theatre roles like Louise in *Carousel* and Luisa in *The Fantasticks* with broad comedies like *Natalie Needs a Nightie* and *Ladies Night in a Turkish Bath.*

Then I saw *A Chorus Line* at the New York Public Theater, and I wanted to be a part of that show. I knew the characters, and I shared their love of dance. In 1976, as *A Chorus Line* swept the Tony Awards, I was in rehearsals at City Center. The original cast (with some substitutions, including me) was going to California. A new cast (with some originals who were not going to California) was going into the Shubert Theatre in New York, and a third company would open in Toronto and then play London. We were all rehearsing together, and the atmosphere sizzled as we competed with our counterparts and cheered each other on. My contract with *A Chorus Line* was for eighteen months, and when it ended, I decided to stay in L.A.

For the next thirteen years, between performances in plays and musicals, I guest starred on television (including *The Facts of Life* with George Clooney), received a Clio nomination for my performance in the Pepsi "Skywriter" commercial, and won the Communications Collaborative Award for the Cleveland Trust commercial, "Ballerina." But I wanted one more dance on Broadway.

In 1989, I attended the Los Angeles auditions for the Broadway production of *Meet Me in St. Louis,* which was based on the Judy Garland film. I was forty-three years old, but I could still play a teenager on stage, and I was hired for the show. Some of the other girls had mothers older than I, so I savored every minute of the run: receiving the Gypsy Robe on opening night, singing and dancing eight shows a week, performing in the Macy's Thanksgiving Day Parade, recording the cast album, joining the Easter Parade with Ivana Trump at the Plaza Hotel, and performing on the Tony Awards. When the show closed, I was given the opportunity to write a television special, and I walked down that new road—a road that eventually brought me back to dance.

At the end of World War II, women were pushed out of the workplace and told that their greatest fulfillment would come from being wives and mothers. Career women virtually disappeared from women's magazines. The ratio of girls to boys in college plummeted, and girls began to marry at a younger age and have more children, but even when I was a child, I could see that people who worked were happier than people who didn't. I could also see that mainstream society was controlled by men who reserved the best jobs for themselves and gave the lower-paying, less-prestigious jobs to women. When I saw my first ballet, I realized that ballet was fundamentally different from the world I knew. At the ballet, women could be the stars.

By the end of the 1960s, when I had established my career on Broadway, the status of women was rising. In the late 1950s, Betty Friedan began to write about the desperate housewives who felt trapped in their homes and were becoming a new class of servant-consumers, and in the early 1960s, her book *The Feminine Mystique* became a bestseller. In 1960, the FDA approved the birth control pill, which allowed women to limit the size of their families without male cooperation. In the mid-1960s, Helen Gurley Brown's *Sex and the Single Girl* and *Sex and the Office* advised young women to get jobs not to snare husbands, but to establish a career, become self-sufficient, and get experience with romance before looking for Mr. Perfect. The Equal Pay Act of 1963 and the Equal Rights Act of 1964 made it illegal for most employers to deny women jobs on the basis of gender or to have two different pay scales, higher for men and lower for women. By 1970, women had many more opportunities than they had had when I was growing up and beginning my career.

Between World War II and 1970, ballet in America was transformed. In the late 1940s and early 1950s, ballet companies, such as Ballet Theatre, Ballet Russe, and the Slavenska-Franklin Ballet, showcased mostly foreign stars and performed one-night stands all around the country. In Wilmington, Delaware, and Oklahoma City, Oklahoma, audiences saw live ballet only when a touring company came to town. Most ballets, even short ballets, had stories, sets, and costumes. Companies were often the passion projects of individuals, and *The Nutcracker* was performed year-round like any other ballet in the repertoire.

By the end of the 1960s, only one great touring company remained, Ballet Theatre, which still employed foreign stars and performed a diverse repertoire. The New York City Ballet had become a first-rate company of mostly American dancers who performed mostly Balanchine ballets. Regional companies had gained traction in Houston, Salt Lake City, and Oklahoma City, and dancers on the East Coast had learned about the San Francisco Ballet, the oldest professional company in the United States. Plotless ballets performed in leotards and tights had come into fashion, and companies had corporate sponsors as well as individual donors. *The Nutcracker* had become a holiday tradition and an important source of revenue for many companies.

The early 1960s were a challenging time to begin a dance career because important ballet companies were disbanding or struggling to survive, and Broadway shows didn't run for decades as some do now, but I had the good fortune to work with some of the great dancers and choreographers of the late twentieth century. I danced in spectacular opera houses and beautiful Broadway theatres. The soundtrack of my life was played by live orchestras, and dance gave me what I wanted most: physical, emotional, and financial freedom; a community that nurtured and inspired me; and an art which nourished my soul. The gifts of dance enrich my life to this day. I still revel in the joy of movement. My perspective has been broadened by travel and by living in a multicultural community, and I have enjoyed a life-long freedom that was denied most women of my mother's generation. At a time when society clipped the wings of women and pushed them into subservient positions, dance allowed women to soar.

What a fascinating flight it has been for me.

Acknowledgments

I am grateful to the many people who made this book possible, beginning with my parents, who introduced me to dance, paid for my lessons, and taught me to forge my own path and follow my dreams. My mother also homeschooled me, which allowed me to graduate from high school at the age of sixteen and tour the world while many of my peers were still in school. My father and my brothers illuminated the chasm between the opportunities for boys and the opportunities for girls during the 1950s.

My formative dance teachers, Anna Marie Leo, Maria Swoboda, James Jamieson, Valentina Pereyaslavec, and Rosella Hightower, were far more than teachers of technique and artistry. They were also dynamic role models who created inspiring communities where young dancers could flourish and grow.

I must also thank the many hundreds of dancers, teachers, choreographers, and writers whose work has enriched my life and added to my knowledge.

Joanne DiVito, Maureen Byrnes, Paulette Fried, and Linda Bunch have been pillars of support at Career Transition for Dancers. Mark Baird guided me through the LEAP (Liberal Education for Arts Professionals) program at St. Mary's College of California, where I conceived *Rebel on Pointe* and wrote the first chapters. The enthusiasm of my fellow students and my teachers in the LEAP program, especially Dr. Jill Nunes-Jensen, Dr. Stuart

Rugg, and Dr. Kathleen Taylor, encouraged me to share my experience with a wider audience.

Jennie Nash at the UCLA Extension Writers' Program advised me during the first draft and led me to Pitchapalooza at {pages} bookstore in Manhattan Beach—an inspiring event that introduced me to Arielle Eckstut and David Henry Sterry, authors of *The Essential Guide to Getting Your Book Published*. Arielle and David helped me polish my proposal and sent it to the acclaimed writer and former New York City Ballet dancer, Toni Bentley, who generously introduced it to the University Press of Florida (UPF).

Meredith Morris-Babb, director of the University Press of Florida, told me clearly and concisely how to make the manuscript better, and her notes greatly improved the book. Meredith Morris-Babb, Arielle Eckstut, David Henry Sterry, Robert Woods, and M. J. Bogatin of Bogatin, Corman, and Gold guided me through the business of publishing.

Mindy Aloff and an anonymous reader for UPF provided additional notes, and their insight and clarity guided my final revisions. Along the way, friends and classmates read various drafts, gave me valuable feedback and encouragement, and shared technical skills and talent: Robert Woods, Pamela Woods-Jackson, Scott Packer, Jeff Copeland, Glenn Shiroma, and Judith Karfiol. I thank Zippora Karz, former New York City Ballet soloist and author of *The Sugarless Plum*, for her early support. For photographs, I thank Lesley Bohm, Bonnefon, Linda Dangcil, Maina Gielgud, Dick Hamilton, Micah Hoggatt at the Houghton Library at Harvard University, Thomas Lisanti at the New York Public Library, Naomi Naughton, Arks Smith, Martha Swope, Joan Weaver, Joseph D. C. Wilson III, and Robert Woods.

Writing this book has been an exciting journey, and I hope that people of all ages, dancers and non-dancers, will enjoy reading it.

Selected Bibliography

Crisp, Clement. "Le Grand Ballet du Marquis de Cuevas." Dance Research: The Journal of the Society for Dance Research 23, no. 1 (2005): 1–17. Accessed July 12, 2012. http://www.euppublishing.com/doi/abs/10.3366./drs.2005.23.1.1.

Dancing for Mr. B: Six Balanchine Ballerinas. Videocassette. Elektra/Wea, 1995.

Garafola, Lynn. *Legacies of Twentieth-Century Dance.* Middletown, Conn.: Wesleyan University Press, 2005.

Hering, Doris. "NYC Ballet . . . Autumn Inventory." *Dance Magazine,* November 1961, 36–37.

Palatsky, Eugene H. "On Their Toes." *Opera News,* April 10, 1965, 12–16.

Tallchief, Maria, with Larry Kaplan. *Maria Tallchief: America's Prima Ballerina.* New York: Henry Holt, 1997.

Terry, Walter. "Bad Deal for Ballet at the Met." *New York World Journal Tribune,* December 4, 1966.

Twenge, Jean M., W. Keith Campbell, and Brittany Gentile. "Male and Female Pronoun Use in U.S. Books Reflects Women's Status, 1900–2008." *Sex Roles* 67, nos. 9–10 (2012):488–93. Abstract. Accessed August 25, 2013. http://link.springer.com/article/10.1007/s11199-012-0194-7.

"Uncertain Future?" *Dance Magazine,* April 1962, 26.

Waiting for Superman trailer. Paramount, 2010. Accessed August 28, 2013. http://www.imdb.com/video/imdb/vi2518550297/.

Index